AMAZING STORIES

ON THEIR
OWN TERMS
True Stories of Trailblazing Women of Vancouver Island

HALEY HEALEY

For my parents, Cathy and Michael Kuntz

Heritage House Publishing Company Ltd.
heritagehouse.ca

Cataloguing information available from Library and Archives Canada

978-1-77203-325-0 (pbk)
978-1-77203-326-7 (epub)

Edited by Lesley Cameron
Proofread by Anumeha Gokhale
Cover photograph: Self-Portrait by Hannah Maynard. Image F-02852 courtesy of the Royal BC Museum and Archives

The interior of this book was produced on 100% post-consumer recycled paper, processed chlorine free, and printed with vegetable-based inks.

Heritage House gratefully acknowledges that the land on which we live and work is within the traditional territories of the Lkwungen (Esquimalt and Songhees), Malahat, Pacheedaht, Scia'new, T'Sou-ke, and W̱SÁNEĆ (Pauquachin, Tsartlip, Tsawout, Tseycum) Peoples.

We acknowledge the financial support of the Government of Canada through the Canada Book Fund (CBF) and the Canada Council for the Arts, and the Province of British Columbia through the British Columbia Arts Council and the Book Publishing Tax Credit.

24 23 22 21 20   1 2 3 4 5

Printed in Canada

Contents

INTRODUCTION 3

CHAPTER 1 HANNAH MAYNARD:
POLICE PHOTOGRAPHER
AND ENTREPRENEUR 7

CHAPTER 2 AGNES DEANS CAMERON:
TEACHER, PRINCIPAL, AND
ARCTIC EXPLORER 15

CHAPTER 3 EMILY CARR: PAINTER AND WRITER 22

CHAPTER 4 VICTORIA WILSON: AVIARY OWNER 29

CHAPTER 5 WYLIE BLANCHET:
SAILOR AND WRITER 33

CHAPTER 6 MARY ANN GYVES (TUWA'HWIYE
TUSIUM GOSSELIM): SALT SPRING
ISLAND PIONEER 38

CHAPTER 7 KIMIKO MURAKAMI: FARMER AND
INTERNMENT CAMP SURVIVOR 42

CHAPTER 8 JOSEPHINE TILDEN: MARINE
BIOLOGIST AND SEASIDE RESEARCH
STATION FOUNDER 49

CHAPTER 9 DOROTHY BLACKMORE: MASTER
MARINER AND MARINE ENGINEER 55

CHAPTER 10   EMMA STARK:
              PIONEER AND TEACHER 60

CHAPTER 11   ALOHA WANDERWELL:
              DRIVER AND PHOTOGRAPHER 66

CHAPTER 12   ADA ANNIE RAE-ARTHUR:
              BACKCOUNTRY ENTREPRENEUR,
              GARDENER, AND BOUNTY HUNTER 72

CHAPTER 13   ANN ELMORE HAIG-BROWN: LIBRARIAN
              AND SOCIAL ADVOCATE 81

CHAPTER 14   ELIZABETH QUOCKSISTER: CULTURAL
              TEACHER AND PHOTOGRAPHER 91

CHAPTER 15   LILIAN BLAND:
              AVIATRIX AND JOURNALIST 98

CHAPTER 16   GA'AXSTA'LAS (JANE CONSTANCE
              COOK): LAND CLAIMS ACTIVIST
              AND TRANSLATOR/INTERPRETER 105

CHAPTER 17   ELLEN GIBBS: CAPE SCOTT PIONEER . . 114

CONCLUSION 122

BIBLIOGRAPHY AND REFERENCES 124

ACKNOWLEDGEMENTS 135

INDEX 137

Introduction
Dare to Become Wild
and Authentic

"Women have always been an equal part of
the past. We just haven't been a part of history."

GLORIA STEINEM

VANCOUVER ISLAND IS a fabulously diverse place. Outwardly
sedate in some areas, and wild, untamed, and unpredictable in
others. Varied in terms of landscape, settlements, ecosystems, and
the people who call it home. Much has been written about the
people who played a significant role in the Island's history. But if
you look at the history books, you'll notice that most of the star-
ring roles are occupied by men, usually of European origin.

Wild places and wild people have always captivated me. I am
happiest while adventuring in untamed places: being thrown from
a horse near Tibet; watching a pack of wolves run toward me on
northern Vancouver Island; playing the fiddle in northern Yukon
and paddling my canoe to the Arctic Ocean through rapids and
untouched black spruce forests. But I first found myself seriously
wondering about the untold stories of the women of Vancouver
Island while touring Cougar Annie's garden after a backcountry

hiking trip. Cougar Annie was a backcountry gardener, wilderness entrepreneur, and cougar bounty hunter who lived near Tofino, BC, in the early 1900s. It delighted me to think of this tiny, feisty woman in gumboots not only convincing the Canadian government to open a post office on her remote and isolated homestead, but also raising eleven children, running a mail-order nursery, outliving four husbands, and carving a productive backcountry garden deep in the rainforest. Her resourcefulness and entrepreneurial nature piqued my curiosity and earned my utmost admiration. She was the epitome of a wild woman, and I wanted to know more.

That's when I started searching for other wild women of Vancouver Island. It turned out there were many more. Women who ranked alongside Cougar Annie in spirit, but whose stories had been lost or forgotten or overlooked. I was flabbergasted. How had I not heard of the sixteen-year-old who was the first female to drive around the world? The first official photographer with the Victoria Police Department? Or the Quatsino Sound homesteader who built and flew her own plane?

The more I discovered, the more I couldn't stop thinking about these wild women and how I felt swindled that I hadn't learned about their stories. Some, like Emily Carr and Cougar Annie, were household names on Vancouver Island. Others, like Kimiko Murakami and Elizabeth Quocksister, had not been formally written about in books or articles and were known to only a handful of people. I wanted to remedy that oversight.

This book contains the profiles of seventeen wild women who opted to challenge the norms, conventions, and expectations of their time and class, or who found themselves with no choice but to follow a path deemed suitable only for men. I chose to write about a variety of women. Some were gentle in their wildness, discreet in their rebellion, while others were more flamboyant. All were dauntless in their quest to achieve their goals. Most importantly, though, they were individuals. All the women I have profiled gave themselves permission to act authentically and let go of what society expected them to be. They set their own standards.

Many of the women I chose to include faced significant setbacks or hardships. When Capi Blanchet's husband died, she rented out her house and took her children and dog sailing up and down Vancouver Island's east coast. Dorothy Blackmore challenged laws that prevented her from becoming a master mariner because she was a woman. Ga'axsta'las fiercely advocated for women and children during a time when Indigenous cultural practices were under threat. These women didn't let grief, difficult circumstances, disability, injustices, or tragic events stop them from living their lives boldly. Perhaps some of us can relate to some of their challenges— and learn from how they dealt with them.

I noted earlier that many of the women's stories were essentially lost or hidden. For my research, I headed to government archives, libraries, museums, newspaper archives, and, of course, the Internet. Whenever possible, I interviewed the woman's family to get the most accurate story. Sometimes there was a wealth of information; other times not so much. At times while researching and writing about a woman, I felt like I was getting to know a new friend, slowly discovering new and interesting things about them as the research revealed their life experiences. I loved them even more as I saw their flaws and vulnerabilities. Their quirky imperfections were endearing. By the time I submitted my first draft to Heritage House, I felt deeply connected to them.

Perhaps you will start with the first story that catches your eye. Or maybe you'll start at the beginning and read them in order—I opted to order them geographically from south to north. Either way, I hope you enjoy their stories as much as I did.

Note of Reconciliation

THIS BOOK WAS written on the traditional and unceded territory of the Snuneymuxw First Nation. Some of the women featured in this book were settlers and newcomers to the area we now call Vancouver Island, but I do not condone colonization or any of the shameful behaviours that came with it. I have chosen to feature a selection of women whose traits and stories sparked my interest. I hope to convey their bravery and uniqueness by sharing their stories. I fully and completely support reconciliation in all its forms and recognize my own role in reconciliation.

1

Hannah Maynard
Police Photographer and Entrepreneur

IT IS 1898, and you enter a building off Johnson Street in Victoria, BC. You walk through a shoe shop on street level, walk up a staircase to the second floor, and pull back a black velvet curtain. Welcome to Hannah Maynard's Photographic Gallery.

On one wall is a penny-farthing bicycle, its large and small wheels leaning against a backdrop of a canoe floating in glassy water. Another wall holds a false fireplace and an emerald-green sofa with a pillow showing the face of a young girl. The smell of sulphur and sandalwood fills your nostrils. A tall vase with a dieffenbachia plant is held up by a cherub statue. A delicate paper parasol hangs above two framed photos: one of a glamorous woman in a black dress, the other of a cemetery headstone. A round table is set for tea with a soft, grey fur rug beneath it. A desk has some papers neatly stacked on it. A large black box with a hole in its front sits on the desk. This is most definitely the workspace

Hannah Maynard in Beacon Hill Park. IMAGE F-05070
COURTESY OF ROYAL BC MUSEUM AND ARCHIVES

of a photographer who created creative, progressive, and unusual photographs.

Hannah Maynard was an unusual woman who did unusual things and lived a remarkably unusual life. She loved bicycles and playing with photographic illusion techniques. Many of her photographic subjects were criminals, as she was the first official photographer of the Victoria Police Department. Hannah Maynard was unapologetically weird and wonderful.

HANNAH HATHERLY MAYNARD was born in Cornwall, England, in 1834. She married her childhood sweetheart, Richard Maynard, in 1852 when she was eighteen and he twenty. They sailed to Canada that year and lived in southern Ontario's Bowmanville, where they owned a leather and shoe store and had three children. Richard soon left to seek gold in the Fraser River gold rush. In his absence, Hannah ran the shoe store and raised their three young children alone. In the little spare time she had, she learned the brand-new technology of the day: photography. She saw it as a business opportunity in days when personal photographers didn't yet exist, and paintings were still the way to capture moments visually. In 1862, the entire Maynard family moved to Victoria, chasing the business opportunities of the west.

Victoria, BC, was a gold rush town. Five blocks in size, it had a Hudson's Bay Company post, tents, saloons, and wooden sidewalks; muddy trails masqueraded as roads. Swamps surrounded the town. Picture a typical Western movie with Victoria as the backdrop. Victoria was booming and there were opportunities to be had. Hannah wasted no time in opening Mrs. R. Maynard's Photographic Gallery on Johnson Street. Photography was now in high demand and the people of Victoria were an ideal target market.

Gold rush towns were teeming with the wealthy and adventurous. Portraiture was becoming increasingly trendy as it was less expensive than paintings, not to mention novel. People wanted their photos taken to keep for themselves, to give to sweethearts, or to send to family far away. Of course, people also wanted photos of their children. Hannah's business plan was solid.

The subjects of her photographs were as wildly diverse as the people living in Victoria at that time—miners, servants, prostitutes, Hudson's Bay Company employees, sailors from the Esquimalt navy base, immigrants, and Indigenous people; rich, poor, criminal, and royalty—they all had photos taken by Hannah, albeit in varying circumstances. One portrait shows a wealthy woman with her small dog, another the blank face of a criminal just charged with theft. Lady Amelia Connolly Douglas, wife of BC's first governor, James Douglas, was photographed by Hannah. She is portrayed sitting regally in a high-backed chair of carved wood and fine upholstery.

Eventually business at Mrs. R. Maynard's Photographic Gallery had boomed to the point where she required an assistant. It was then that her husband, Richard, who had been operating a shoe store below her studio, joined her photographic business.

Hannah, whose studio logo referred to her as a "photographic artist," taught Richard all she knew, and he opened a small photo salon on the ground floor behind his shoe store. Although their photography business would soon out-earn Richard's shoe business, he seems to have been a pragmatic man with a measured approach to risk taking as he kept the shoe business as a going concern.

By then, photography was also in high demand elsewhere in BC, so Richard went travelling while Hannah focused on the Victoria market. Richard's photography took him to the Nanaimo River, Barkerville, the Cariboo, northern BC, and Yukon Territory. In 1892 he photographed an investigation of seal hunting in Alaska. Many of his photos featured landscapes of mining and the new Canadian Pacific Railroad. Hannah would sometimes join him if her studio wasn't too busy. Together, they explored Banff, Bute Inlet, and Haida Gwaii. The two were a powerful pair. Together and apart they produced stunning photographs.

The Maynard Photographic Gallery had three different homes, moving as it expanded. The first was at Johnson and Douglas Streets. The second was in the same area but was bigger and boasted a larger sign. The last move was to 41 Pandora Street, where they sold cameras, leathers, and shoes—a rather odd combination of goods to be sold together, but a true blending of their business interests.

PROFESSIONAL PHOTOGRAPHY WAS an unusual profession for a woman in Hannah's day. Some people boycotted Mrs. R. Maynard's Photographic Gallery, not wanting to support a female business owner. But Hannah persevered. She kept at her trade and continued pushing the limits of photography. When Richard was taking photographs out of town, Hannah's studio in Victoria was busy enough for her to hire an assistant named Arthur Rappertie, who worked for her between 1882 and 1904.

Innovation is evident in all of Hannah's work. She experimented with cutting-edge photographic techniques her entire career. Image manipulation, mirrors, masking, and multiple exposure were just a few of these techniques. She also used photosculpture, composite images, multiple exposures, cut-and-paste montage, and the illusion of movement in photographs. She did several rare bas-relief photos, building up the subject's features using blotting paper and a bone paper knife and filling it in with papier mâché. Hannah loved self-portraits and composite images, showing the same subject multiple times. One photo shows five Hannahs in a row. Another, a multiple exposure photograph, playing with trick photography and poking fun at the ritual of teatime, shows three Hannahs: one sitting at a table pouring tea, and one looking at the camera from a picture frame on the wall, pouring milk on the head of a third Hannah. For the time, this was seriously innovative. Hannah's quirky, dry sense of humour came through in her bizarre photosculpture photos of herself and her grandson

Maynard McDonald. Maynard lived with Hannah after his mother drowned, and because his father, Hannah's son, was an alcoholic. Photosculpture photography, which had emerged in the late 1800s, involved dressing the subject in white, covering their skin in white powder, and putting a black drop cloth over their lower body or arms, truncating the body to make ghostly white "spirit creatures." One of Hannah's photosculptures showed a girl smiling, then the same girl crying. Some found photosculptures creepy, especially ones depicting truncated children.

Hannah played with the roots of modern airbrushing and digital retouching. In her self-portraits of her later years, she removed wrinkles from her face, lightened the skin on her face, and adjusted her waistline to give herself an hourglass shape. Her playful attitude toward reality and illusion made her photos haunting and unique. In today's world of camera phones and filter apps, these techniques may not seem remarkable, but in her day, they were groundbreaking. Few photographers at that time were using the techniques she had mastered.

Hannah was a quintessential artist. She lived as she pleased. She spoke quickly and in short phrases more than complete sentences. She had an energetic curiosity about the world around her and her surroundings. High-spirited and determined in all she did, her style of dress was as unique as her photographs. She dressed flamboyantly, with brightly coloured full-skirted gowns, hats hung with feathers or flowers, and long embroidered gloves, and wore her hair in tight curls, contrasting with the long ringlets many women wore at the time.

She also had a special knack for taking children's photos. Unlike other photographers of the time, who used a stick to prop children up rigidly, she let children be relaxed and comfortable and in whatever position they liked. The result was photos that were natural, candid, and distinctive. Each Christmas, Hannah made photo collages of all the children's faces she had photographed that year. The collage was tintype gem style and displayed the faces uniquely, on a vase or the leaves of a plant, in strange diamond shapes or on a shimmering abalone shell. Each child's mother would receive a copy of this *Gems of British Columbia* print.

In 1887 Hannah's career took an exciting turn. She became the first official photographer for the Victoria Police Department. Criminals of all sorts came to her studio for mug shots. Many had committed minor offences like stealing, but others, like Belle Adams, had committed serious crimes. Belle murdered her lover while trying to decapitate him with a razor blade. Hannah cleverly used a mirror to get a full-face mug shot and a profile on the same negative. She became good at split-lighting techniques for portraits and would sometimes place a mirror at people's feet to create the illusion of them sitting near water. Her position as official police photographer rewarded Hannah for her talent and intelligence.

After her youngest daughter, Lillie, died of typhoid fever in 1883, Hannah became very interested in death and the afterworld. The photograph on the pillow of her parlour sofa showed Lillie. When her son Albert's wife drowned, Hannah hung a photo of her in her parlour. She joined the trendy spiritualism movement, attending picnics and séances with a group in Victoria.

Hannah also enjoyed bicycling and managed to combine this hobby with photography. She rode bikes with her grandson Maynard around Beacon Hill Park. This was a popular Victoria activity. Hannah would also go to the park and photograph people on bicycles, trying to make them look as if they were moving even when still. She used people on bicycles to experiment with the illusion of movement when the bicycle was standing still.

In 1907 Richard Maynard died in Victoria. Hannah continued her photography work for five years after his death. When she retired in 1912, it wasn't because she was tired of it, but because she wanted to give the younger generation of photographers a chance. Her son Albert took over the family photography company. An eclectic fellow, his other careers included being a professional dancer, magician, gun collector, circus acrobat, ornithologist, and taxidermist for the Royal BC Museum.

IN 1918 EIGHTY-FIVE-YEAR-OLD Hannah Maynard died unexpectedly. She was buried in her family plot in Victoria's Ross Bay Cemetery.

Hannah Maynard was a stunning original—the late-1800s version of an early adopter of technology. It was remarkable enough to be a female business owner in her time, but particularly remarkable was her progressive experimentation with photographic techniques. She constantly pushed the limits and experimented with photographic techniques; she was decades ahead of her time. And yet, despite the complexity and unprecedented nature of her work, it has gone largely unrecognized. Hannah Maynard, a talented and creative photographer who created whimsical, eerie, haunting photos that are eye-catching to this day, is a surprisingly unknown figure today.

2

Agnes Deans Cameron
Teacher, Principal, and Arctic Explorer

AGNES DEANS CAMERON was captivated by Canada's North. She travelled overland to the Arctic Ocean and introduced Canadians to the North through her photos, lectures, and book. If that wasn't enough, Agnes was the first female high school teacher and first high school principal in the city of Victoria. She's remembered best, though, for her fight for equal pay for female teachers.

AGNES DEANS CAMERON was born in Victoria, BC, in 1863. She was the youngest of six children whose parents had emigrated separately from Scotland, met in California, and moved to Victoria. The Victoria of Agnes's childhood was a bustling gold rush town filled with opportunities and passionate, driven people. Agnes's family lived in a house that they built themselves on what is now Government Street, near Emily Carr's childhood home.

Always a lover of learning, Agnes attended public elementary school and the first public high school in British Columbia. She became a teacher when she was only sixteen years old, while still completing her own high school education. BC had recently initiated the *Public School Act* and was desperate for new teachers. She wrote and passed the exam that allowed her to become a teacher, noting critically, after speaking to her male peers afterward, that the exam questions differed according to the sex of the student.

Agnes's first teaching assignment was in 1879 at Angela's College, a private girls' school run by the Church of England. Her second was in Comox in 1882, where she had to walk along the estuary to get to her one-room schoolhouse. After that, she taught in Granville and then finally back in Victoria, eventually becoming Victoria's first female high school teacher in 1890 and its first female principal in 1894.

Far from being an average teacher, Agnes is remembered as competent and engaging. Former students recall her passion and ability to instill a genuine joy of learning. Along with her passion came the uninhibited expression of her own views, some of which were viewed as contentious for the time. In her students, she wanted to promote self-esteem, good citizenship, and social responsibility. She valued analytical skills over home economics, industrial arts, and agricultural training. She believed students should be educated in a liberal manner, developing analytical critical thinking skills and problem-solving abilities rather than vocational skills specific to one job. In writing about her opinion of the school curriculum to parents and teachers she said, "Don't strive to fashion your children into one stereotyped pattern. A child's individuality is the divine spark in him. Let it burn."

Agnes Deans Cameron

Agnes Deans Cameron and Jessie Brown at
Peace River camp, Alberta 1908. IMAGE M07367
COURTESY OF CITY OF VICTORIA ARCHIVES

But, like most of her peers, Agnes believed in corporal punishment and using the strap. In 1906 she used the strap on a male student she saw as needing disciplining, and the boy's father subsequently complained. The matter went to the school board and she was reprimanded. She later failed to comply with educational policies regarding examinations and was reprimanded again. She and an art teacher allowed their students to use rulers in a freehand drawing exercise, a move that resulted in her teaching degree being revoked. Her career had been of the utmost importance to her. She was a third-generation teacher, following in the footsteps of her mother and maternal grandmother. Teaching had been her passion and vocation for twenty-five years. That same year, her mother passed away.

Despite losing her teaching job and her mother, Agnes powered on. She was voted school trustee by the most votes. She also switched careers, becoming a journalist and writing specifically about educational reform and gender equality issues. She moved briefly to Chicago, where she worked as a writer and editor before being hired by the Dominion government to promote the settlement of remote areas of western Canada. She was thrilled by the assignment and jumped in wholeheartedly.

As part of the position, Agnes and her niece Jessie Cameron Brown embarked on an epic journey to northern Canada: a six-month trip covering 16,000 kilometres. They followed fur trade routes down the Athabasca and Mackenzie Rivers until they reached the Arctic Ocean. Her job: to portray the area attractively using words and photos to lure new settlers to the land, which was intensely remote and mostly inhabited by Indigenous people and very few trappers, fur traders, prospectors, or missionaries.

Agnes and Jessie set off on their daring expedition in May 1908. Their luggage was minimal: a tent, two steamer trunks, two cameras, a typewriter, two raincoats, two blankets, a thin waterproof mattress, and a "Hudson's Bay suitcase" (a flour bag holding tent poles, wash basin, and hatchet). The women travelled by rail, stagecoach, steamer, and sturgeon-head scow—a large, sturdy boat used for river and lake travel, and a regular means of transport for Hudson's Bay Company employees. They portaged their gear around rapids and alongside the men on the expedition. They identified hot pink fireweed, blue harebells, and the orchid-like pink lady's slippers. They saw hundreds of the endangered wood buffalo, white pelican, Arctic terns, and muskox. One day, Agnes shot a two hundred-kilogram moose, which they cooked over a campfire and ate. They saw ochre and tar on the banks of the Athabasca River, and became intimately acquainted with mosquitos.

The North, including the lives of its residents, captivated Agnes: the fiddle music at night, bannock instead of bread, the eerie and stimulating midnight sun, the sweet smell of wild roses, and the glimpse she got into the lives of Hudson's Bay Company fur traders. She was in her element, free from city conventions and clad in a police-style broad-rimmed hat, shortened dress, and loose-fitting coat.

Upon returning from the North, and following the publication of a book titled *The New North,* Agnes became a celebrity. She gave talks in Canada and the UK about her trip to northern Canada to promote emigration to Canada's North.

Her insights about the North were astute and sharp-witted. Her description of gold rush madness captured it all beautifully: "Gold-fever is a disease without diagnosis or doctor—infectious, contagious, and hereditary; if its germ once stirs in a man's blood, till the day of his death he is not immune from an attack. The discovery of gold-dust in Dawson sent swarming through the waterways of sub-Arctic Canada a heterogeneous horde—gamblers of a hundred hells, old-time miners from quiet firesides, beardless boys from their books, human parasites of two continents, and dreamers from the Seven Seas."

Her photos and writing were incredibly well-received. During a civic reception held for her in a city ballroom, she was given accolades for her contribution to Victoria: "From infancy to womanhood, you have been associated with the development and intellectual life of the city."

AFTER CONTRACTING PNEUMONIA following an appendectomy, Agnes Deans Cameron passed away in May of 1912. She was forty-nine. Hers was the largest funeral procession Victoria had ever seen and the *Daily Colonist* wrote impressively about her: "It is possible that when the history of British Columbia comes to be written the name of Agnes Deans Cameron will be inscribed therein as the most remarkable woman citizen of British Columbia, and her story will stand out all the more prominently in as much as her death occurred when she appeared to be at the very zenith of her career, with a brilliant future ahead of her."

Agnes Deans Cameron was self-reliant, strong, and savvy. At the time of her death, she was a famous Canadian writer and a member of the Women's Press Club, Society for the Prevention of Cruelty of Animals, Children's Aid Society, Dominion Women's Enfranchisement Association, and Local Council of Women in Victoria and Vancouver Island.

She lived an uncommon lifestyle for her day, forgoing marriage and motherhood for a career and backcountry expeditions. She was the first non-Indigenous woman to reach the Arctic Ocean by land. She was smart, stubborn, and strong-willed. She was ridiculed for wearing her hair short and for wearing loose-fitting trousers and coats. She wore them anyway.

Agnes constantly criticized educational ideals she saw as outdated. She fought fiercely for women to participate fully and equally in the teaching profession. Her career offered her engagement, challenge, and a way to make a difference.

Humans have always been drawn to danger and adventure, but during Agnes's lifetime, it was almost exclusively men who answered adventure's call. Agnes challenged that, showing that women could answer that call equally loud and clear. The North held her spellbound and kindled her sense of adventure. As only skilled writers and speakers can, Agnes Deans Cameron conveyed the vividness of the North—its unique people, rich cultures, vast land, striking wildflowers, and abundant wildlife—to readers and audiences who would never get to see it for themselves.

3

Emily Carr
Painter and Writer

EMILY CARR DEEPLY adored BC's forests and shorelines. She felt most alive and her best self while she painted with her feet in the sand, breathed salty sea breezes, or walked in calm forest clearings. Trees and waves fuelled her and kindled her creativity. Dynamic movement is felt in her tree paintings, strength is conjured by her totem poles, and people of Vancouver Island related to her painting of two tall trees, standing side by side in a lonely clear-cut, spared from logging. Her paintings draw you in so you are suddenly in a forest of giant trees, or alone on a secluded shoreline, placing you in two places at once: in reality viewing the painting, but also immersed in the painting with strong branches above you or ever-shifting ocean waves undulating in front of you.

EMILY CARR IS a household name on Canada's west coast. A university in Vancouver—Emily Carr University of Art and

Design—bears her name. But her life story is less well known. Like a bold brushstroke on canvas, she painted over societal norms of her time. She devoted her life to her craft of painting rather than marrying and having children, and also had a social justice conscience that put her ahead of her time. She was anti-colonial, criticized the actions of the missionaries of those days, and disapproved of residential schools.

Emily was born in Victoria on December 13, 1871. The second-youngest of nine children, her childhood was spent in Victoria. From a very young age, she loved art, animals, and nature, although she was in her twenties before she picked up a paintbrush. Her parents immigrated to Canada from England, and her father owned a wholesale grocery and liquor store in Victoria that sold supplies to miners during the gold rush. Emily's mother died of tuberculosis in 1886 and her father died in 1888, when Emily was fourteen and sixteen respectively, and her eldest sister then took over the running of the household. When Emily was eighteen, she left Victoria to study art at San Francisco's California School of Design. It was here she fell in love with painting, opening up a new world for her.

Upon returning from San Francisco, Emily taught art classes out of her own studio. In 1898, when she was twenty-seven, she visited her sister in the west coast fishing village of Ucluelet, where she fell in love again. This time it was with an Indigenous approach to life on the traditional territory of the Nuu-chah-nulth Nation. Totem poles especially drew her in. She felt compelled to paint them in their original settings and to document what she saw as a declining way of life, and was enthralled with their representation of family history. Her earliest paintings of them were in cubist style; later, she adopted postmodernist techniques. Many of her

Emily Carr and her animals, including a monkey named Woo.
IMAGE G-00414 COURTESY OF ROYAL BC MUSEUM AND ARCHIVES

most famous pieces feature totem poles, as well as house posts, shoreline villages, and canoes. She painted totem poles from up and down the west coast of BC and Alaska, but her most famous images are the "totem forests" of Haida Gwaii.

When she was twenty-eight, Emily went to England to study art. On her return, she worked as a cartoonist, taught art in Vancouver, and painted in Stanley Park on weekends. She sold her art to make a living and to fund her love of travel. Her art education took her to California, England, and France: She attended the Académie Colarossi in Paris for three months and went to Brittany and Crécy-en-Brie in France. In London, England, she studied at the

Westminster School of Art. But, close to home, the west coast of Vancouver Island may have been her favourite travel destination. She returned to Ucluelet many times, and the west coast Indigenous villages retained a special place in her heart. During one of her Ucluelet trips she was gifted the name of Klee Wyck—Laughing One.

Emily had some major setbacks in her life. The Royal BC Museum would not purchase any of the two hundred paintings she painted over five years after they were shown at a large solo exhibition in Vancouver. They said her style was too modern and they had no interest in celebrating or showcasing Indigenous culture. This was such an enormous blow that Emily painted very little for more than a decade and came close to giving up painting all together.

Isolation was a constant hardship. She had been close to her mother, and after her mother's death, she refused to talk to her father, although no one knows why. Although Emily travelled with her sister Alice, her other sisters were dismissive of her art. She struggled with mental health challenges for much of her adult life, and after a diagnosis of hysteria—an all too common diagnosis imposed on women in those days—she spent a year and a half in a sanatorium in England.

Money was tight throughout Emily's adult life, although she contrived creative ways to make ends meet. She turned her apartment into a boarding house with four suites, although the demotion, as she saw it, from artist to landlady was difficult. She resented the house, the cooking, and the cleaning. But she did what she needed to do to keep painting. At certain points, she raised sheepdogs, rabbits, and chickens in the backyard. Painting was her priority; the other things were simply a means to allow her to keep creating.

Emily's perseverance paid off. In 1927 Eric Brown, director of the National Gallery of Canada, requested Emily's paintings for an art show in Ottawa. Paintings from Group of Seven artists were featured in the same show, and Emily eventually became affiliated with the Group of Seven. For the first time she felt connected and like she belonged. Her paintings were—finally—becoming recognized, a development that she valued more than the idea of her name becoming recognized.

Despite her fierce independence, Emily Carr had mentors, people who informed her work and helped her grow from small-town art creator to famous master artist. James Everett Stuart was an artistic mentor who had a studio in New York. Harry Gibb was a modern painter and a mentor who inspired her to paint with bold and bright colours. A New Zealand painter named Frances Hodgkins was her watercolour teacher in Concarneau, France. Lawren Harris of the Group of Seven was another mentor. He gave her friendship and valuable feedback on her work.

EMILY CARR WAS charmingly eccentric and unafraid to live life unconventionally. She kept rats, dogs, cats, and birds as pets, but her most unusual pet was a monkey named Woo. She would load her family of animals into her trailer, which she called Elephant, and they would drive to Goldstream Park, where Emily would paint in the company of her animals, surrounded by trees and fresh air.

She also embodied the concept of a lifelong learner. Always striving to improve, she was unhappy being stagnant. Her painting style evolved as she travelled, studied, and aged. At sixty-five years old, she was still employing new painting techniques. At seventy, after a second heart attack, she became an author, when her

Emily Carr and her caravan named elephant. IMAGE D-03844
COURTESY OF THE THE ROYAL BC MUSEUM AND ARCHIVES

non-fiction book *Klee Wyck* was published. A memoir about her time spent in Indigenous communities painting totem poles, it later won the Governor General's award, making Emily the second woman ever to win this prestigious award.

In 1945, at seventy-three years old, Emily Carr died of a heart attack. She was buried in Victoria's Ross Bay in her family plot. A large family headstone marks her parents' and three sisters' graves; a simple granite stone marks Emily's. It reads:

Emily Carr
1871–1945
Artist and Author
Lover of Nature

Loyal fans have left her gifts. Paintbrushes, pencils, beads, stones, and artworks brighten up the simple stone. In 2001 a larger headstone that displays Emily's writing was added. The piece chosen perfectly depicts her deep, unwavering love of nature:

Dear mother earth!
I think I have always specially belonged to you.
I have loved from babyhood to roll upon you, to lie with my face pressed right down onto you in my sorrows.
I love the look of you and the smell of you and the feel of you.
When I die I should like to be in you unconfined, unshrouded, the petals of flowers against my flesh and you covering me up.

Emily Carr left an enduring legacy. After her death, Victoria got a public art gallery—something Emily had wanted for years. A bronze statue of Emily stands by the Victoria waterfront. It depicts her sitting sketching with her monkey, Woo, and her dog, Billie. Emily Carr University of Art and Design was established in 1925 and nurtures hundreds of aspiring artists annually. Her house, 207 Government Street in Victoria, contains authentic furnishings from her childhood and is open to visitors.

Emily was a young soul who embraced change. A Canadian icon and the only woman to be directly associated with the prestigious Group of Seven. She loved the west coast. She lived life wild and in solitude. She loved trees, totem poles, shorelines, nature, and freedom—all poignantly depicted in her famous paintings.

4

Victoria Wilson
Aviary Owner

THE SAD AND elegant woman perched on a soft antique chair, sipping a cup of steaming hot tea while gazing around her large and luxurious house. An enormous crystal chandelier hung above her, shimmering and refracting bright afternoon light onto the intricately sculptured ceilings and fine furniture that adorned her sitting room. Beyond the sitting room, rooms held closets bursting with her shopping treasures: fashionable dresses, never-worn hats still in their boxes, fine women's gloves, and an impressive collection of sweet-smelling perfumes.

Despite her lavish living quarters and abundant hauls from frequent shopping trips, a wave of loneliness engulfed her. She got up gracefully from the antique armoire chair and walked lightly up the hand-carved spiral staircase. At the top of the stairs she caught her breath, feeling better, knowing she was close to a visit with her true loves. She opened a large glass door and stepped into her

Victoria Wilson's Burdett Avenue "Parrot House."
COURTESY OF T.W. PATERSON

aviary. The cheerful chirping of her many birds welcomed her, and her loneliness dissipated as she looked around at her more than sixty beloved birds: lovebirds, budgies, pheasants, macaws, and her favourite—Louis the parrot. The bright light coming in through the aviary windows added to her improving mood. Beyond her grounds lay the familiar sight of her city: Victoria, BC. But she was content to be inside, the thought of the world outside bringing on a sense of unease.

VICTORIA JANE WILSON was born in Victoria, BC, in 1878. Her mother was from a family of fur traders, originally from England; her father was a wealthy banker and real estate broker from Scotland. The family home was a lavish three-storey, white mansion with a turret at 730 Burdett Avenue in Victoria. Victoria's upbringing was secluded and restricted due to her strict, overprotective father who forbade her from socializing, and she became increasingly reclusive throughout her life.

Victoria enjoyed painting, drawing, and horse riding, but birds and shopping were her favourite hobbies. Her bird collecting began when her father gave her a brilliant blue and yellow macaw for her fifth birthday. Throughout the years, she acquired more and more birds, until she had sixty different kinds. The entire top storey of the mansion was an aviary—one of the largest in the city at that time. She had budgies, peach-faced lovebirds, Panamanian parrots, and Mexican yellow-headed parrots, but Louis the macaw was her favourite. She bought an electric car so she could take him for car rides. The driving lessons that purchase necessitated would have been quite an undertaking for someone so introverted and reclusive. As it turned out, the fumes irritated Louis' skin and the noise bothered him, so the car was a short-lived endeavour. She later bought Louis his own parrot, who was forty years younger than Louis and whom she named Morrie. She had a single cat, which, it can only be assumed, was kept out of the aviary. Victoria paid no attention to societal norms in terms of how many pets were considered appropriate and housed as many animals as she pleased.

Shopping was her other interest. But she didn't buy just one of her choices; she bought many. She bought hats, gloves, and perfume in bulk. When she died, over a hundred pairs of white gloves and other unworn clothes were found in her mansion. The electric automobile she bought was barely used, with less than one charge on it.

Victoria was very shy and rarely left the house. On the rare occasions that she did attend social events, she was said to hover in the corner of the room and talked very little. In hindsight, it looks as if Victoria struggled with mental health challenges at a time when such challenges were poorly understood and not talked about. Her mother died in 1917, when Victoria was forty. Her father died in 1934. Her reclusiveness worsened with these losses.

VICTORIA DIED IN 1949 at the age of seventy-two from pneumonia. Her name could have been forgotten if it weren't for her will—which quite literally went to the birds. Although she left a generous sum of money to the Red Cross, several hospitals, and an orphanage, she also left a large amount to Louis the macaw. Strict instructions accompanied the large sum for his care. The will stated that her trusted gardener, Yue Wah Wong, would care for Louis and that he would receive a generous stipend of $200 (the equivalent of over $2,000 in today's money) a week for this. Her mansion could be sold, but not developed, while Louis was still alive. Louis was living on prime real estate. He outlived Yue, who died in 1967, and was then looked after by Yue's family until his death in 1985. He was 115 years of age. He was a celebrity around Victoria by this time and was even featured in *Life* magazine. He had lived a life of luxury, with a full-time caretaker who fed him hard-boiled eggs, walnuts, and brandy.

The land where Victoria and Louis lived now houses the Chateau Victoria Hotel. Their legacy lives on through names like Victoria Jane's for the bar and The Parrot House Restaurant over the years. The hotel is one of the city's haunted places, with people reporting ghostly sightings of Victoria, doors opening and closing on their own, and elevator buttons lighting up without being touched. Victoria was an eccentric character who certainly lived life her own way.

5

Wylie Blanchet
Sailor and Writer

IT WAS A sunny summer morning and the children weren't yet awake. The Captain sat in the wheelhouse of her twenty-five-foot sailboat. This was her favourite time of day: the time of quiet, of glassy calm seas, writing, coffee, and dreamy thoughts. Her sailboat was moored in a calm bay, light waves lapping at the sides. She drank in the tangy smell of the sea at low tide and the decadent aroma of fresh coffee from the steaming mug in her hand. Early morning mist shrouded the green mountains out the window, an eagle glided over the boat, and her five children slept soundly in their designated places.

The Captain sipped her coffee and wrote in a weathered notebook before the children awoke and they began another day of cruising the inside coast of Vancouver Island.

The Captain was Wylie Blanchet, or "Capi." She was a coastal explorer, writer, and mother of five. She refused to let difficult circumstances stop her from enjoying life fully.

WYLIE BLANCHET WAS born Muriel W. Liffiton in Montreal, Quebec, in 1892. She was the second of three daughters and was a talented rower. In 1909 she married a banker named Geoffrey Blanchet. He was twenty-three and she was eighteen. They lived in Sherbrooke, Toronto, and finally Saanich, when Geoffrey retired early due to health problems. The family bought a cabin on Curteis Point in Saanich that they called Little House. They also bought a twenty-five-foot motor boat named *The Caprice*.

Five years after moving to Little House, Geoffrey drowned while out on a solo sailing trip. Capi, as she preferred to be known, found herself a widow at just thirty-four. For income, she wrote articles. This allowed her to be home to care for her children, who were homeschooled. They spent the four warmer months of the year boating on *The Caprice* while their home was rented out to generate extra money. Their dog, a Gordon setter named Pam, rode in a dinghy they towed behind them. Although it was crowded at night, the boat was spacious in the daytime when everything was stowed away tidily. Capi recorded the stories of their coastal travels in her now famous book, *The Curve of Time*.

Capi and her children explored places most people (locals and tourists alike) had never been. Following Captain Vancouver's routes, they explored Kingcome Inlet, Seymour Inlet, Jervis Inlet, Desolation Sound, Quadra Island, Cortes Island, Mistaken Island off Nanoose Bay, and the Skookumchuck Rapids. Whenever she could, Capi wrote about their time on the boat.

Capi Blanchet. COURTESY OF MICHAEL, JANET, AND TARA BLANCHET

Boat life was memorable. They fished in streams with unripe huckleberries that resembled salmon eggs. They tracked weather by clouds and a barometer. They showered in waterfalls, washed dishes in the ocean, and cooked salmon on beach bonfires. They rarely knew what day of the week it was. Some nights they fell asleep under star-filled skies.

They saw Kwakwaka'wakw longhouses with intricate carvings of ravens holding up enormous beams. From their boat they saw shell midden beaches, Kwakwaka'wakw people fishing in cedar dugout canoes, and burial trees hung with coffins held up by cedar ropes. They explored backcountry trapper cabins and visited eccentric pioneers.

Challenges were plentiful, though. Capi navigated *The Caprice* through wind, waves, currents, fog, tides, rain, and ocean swell. She diagnosed engine issues and made decisions about their route. She navigated through island mazes, occasionally enlisting help from her oldest daughter and son.

When her children were grown and the years of cruising the coast by boat were behind her, Capi settled down at Little House. Little House was perched high up on a hill above the ocean, where gulls and cormorants flew, the sound and sight of the tides offered constant comfort, and winter storms could be watched from above. The house stood in an arbutus and Douglas fir forest. When it became too rundown to live in any more, in 1945, Capi's son David built her a modern bungalow.

Capi loved writing and spent much time in her later years writing a book about her travels up and down the coast with her children. In 1962 the same year that she died, Blackwood & Sons, a Scottish publishing company, printed seven hundred copies of *The Curve of Time*. It wasn't wildly popular or well distributed, but it chronicled the family's adventures and Capi proudly gave a copy to each of her children. On September 29, 1961, Capi was found lying dead over her typewriter. She was sixty-nine years old and had suffered a stroke while working on her second book. She left the physical world doing what she loved: writing.

CAPI'S POPULARITY AS a writer gained steam after her death. In 1962 *The Curve of Time* was picked up and co-published by Gray's Publishing and Whitecap Books. This time, the book was welcomed like waves to a beach. It continues to be popular today, especially among seafarer folk and coastal dwellers. Then, in 1982, a children's book Capi had written with her children in the 1930s was published. *A Whale Named Henry* told of an orca who was trapped in an inlet near the Skookumchuck Rapids and befriended a seagull named Timothy who had a broken wing. Timothy's character was inspired by a seagull the children had found in the garden at Little House. Capi's children went on to become an architect, artist, geological engineer, romance novelist, and nurse.

Capi loved exploring and writing. She is better known now than when she was alive. Each year more visitors and locals read her exciting accounts of boating along the BC coast. Her words and stories look likely to endure for many decades.

6

Mary Ann Gyves (Tuwa'hwiye Tusium Gosselim)
Salt Spring Island Pioneer

THERE IS A sparkling cove on Salt Spring Island's western shore called Burgoyne Bay. Located between the mouths of two creeks, it is sheltered from the rough seas that surround the island. In Hul'qumi'num, Burgoyne Bay is called Hwaaqwum, or place of the sawbill ducks. A place of abundant food, it had sawbill ducks, clam beds, herring, streams teaming with coho and chum salmon, and camas fields. Artifacts aged by archaeologists have shown that Cowichan Coast Salish people have been using Burgoyne Bay for over three thousand years. Burgoyne Bay is also where Mary Ann Gyves was born and raised.

Mary Ann Gyves (Tuwa'hwiye Tusium Gosselim)

MARY ANN GYVES (Tuwa'hwiye Tusium Gosselim) was born around 1854 at Burgoyne Bay, Salt Spring Island. One of three children, her father was George Tusilum, a Cowichan Chieftain; her mother, a daughter of the Clem-Klemulutz Clan, was named Taltunaat. As a girl, Mary Ann collected plants—including salmonberries, button-berries, and Oregon grape shoots—in a woven cedar basket. A healer from a young age, she learned midwifery from her Cowichan family and later delivered many babies on Salt Spring Island.

In July 1886 Mary Ann married Michael Gyves, one of Salt Spring Island's original settlers. Intermarriage between people of different ethnic backgrounds was commonplace and accepted on Salt Spring Island. Michael had left his home country of Ireland when he was eighteen, for New York; he then worked for the US army on the San Juan Islands for five years. Gold fever took him to the Cariboo region of BC. Upon finding no gold, he returned to the coast, where he met a man named John Maxwell in Victoria. John spoke of Salt Spring Island's fertile valleys, healthy fish populations, forests full of wood, and perfect pastures for livestock. Michael was sold on the idea and moved to Salt Spring Island right away. He pre-empted a few hundred acres of land beside Fulford Creek. Land pre-emptions were bought at $1.25 per acre and married men could pre-empt more than single men. Women, however, were only permitted to pre-empt land if they were widowed with dependents.

The Salt Spring Island forest was extremely dense and had to be cleared before being farmed. The couple worked together to get it ready. To clear stumps, Mary Ann put chains around them, which she attached to a plow. Michael drove the plow until the stumps were removed from the ground, with Mary Ann driving

Mary Ann Gyves holding Bob Akerman. COURTESY OF THE SALT SPRING ISLAND HISTORICAL SOCIETY ARCHIVES—CHARLES KHAN COLLECTION

the oxen that pulled the plow. A stone-boat, a sled-like box, was used to haul away rocks. Wood was saved for barns, houses, and fences. The rest was burned. This method of land clearing—slash and burn—became illegal in the 1920s.

Mary Ann and Michael's land was endowed with giant cedar trees several metres in diameter, and they went into business making cedar shakes from them. There were no roads to get the shakes to the water, and no wharves. In fact, at this point, there were no roads on Salt Spring Island at all. Michael would row the shakes to Sidney or Victoria, to be sold at markets. Although Mary Ann could shoot, when Michael was away from home she preferred to shoo away wild animals with an old broom or large stick. Michael claimed that cougars were more scared of her stick than his gun.

Mary Ann and Michael had three children, Ellen, Michael, and Mary Katherine, who were baptized at St. Paul's Roman Catholic Church in Salt Spring Island's Fulford Harbour. Mary Ann kept her Catholic faith but also maintained her Indigenous culture. She taught her children and grandchildren about her culture and how to speak the Hul'qumi'num language. Her grandson Ted Akerman said she taught residents about traditional foods in the Burgoyne Bay area where she grew up. Bob Akerman remembers his grandmother teaching him about catching and drying fish from the creek, digging and drying clams on the fire, and cultivating the purple-flowered camas bulb, an important food source for the First Nations in the area. She also showed him the red ochre rock that came from Burgoyne Bay and could be rubbed into a fine powder and mixed with oil to be used as paint for ceremonial and ritual purposes.

IN 1941, AT age eighty-seven, Mary Ann died in Fulford Harbour. She and Michael rest in St. Paul's cemetery there. The couple was on Salt Spring Island long before it had ferry service, before Mouat's store, before it was logged, before Mount Maxwell had its name, and before it became a place for artists who had the leisure time for creating art.

Mary Ann's cultural knowledge lives on through her family. For years, her grandson Bob Akerman had a museum filled with Indigenous artifacts, and Bob's grandson Joe Akerman was a carver and cultural teacher who educated others about local Indigenous culture. Mary Ann is remembered as a dedicated grandmother, known as Granny Gyves to non-relatives. She was someone who maintained her culture despite being married to someone from another culture.

7

Kimiko Murakami
Farmer and Internment Camp Survivor

GANBARU IS A Japanese word meaning to slog on tenaciously through hard times, to tough it out and persevere. Kimiko Murakami maintained a *ganbaru* mentality during a time of appalling injustices to Japanese Canadians.

KIMIKO OKANO WAS born in 1904 in Steveston, BC, a coastal village near Vancouver. Both her parents were born in Japan; her father was from a prestigious family and her mother from a samurai family. When Kimiko was five years old, the family moved from Steveston to Salt Spring Island, a gulf island southwest of Vancouver and northeast of Victoria. Japanese Canadians were not permitted to vote or have certain professional jobs at that time, but they could fish, farm, and log.

Kimiko Murakami

On Salt Spring Island, the Okano family fished. From a very young age, Kimiko would drive boats to deliver fish from Salt Spring Island to Vancouver. After her younger sister drowned and the family's houseboat was destroyed by fire, the family briefly returned to Japan. When her mother and father returned to Salt Spring Island to fish, they left Kimiko and her surviving sister in Japan. Kimiko excelled at academics and music, but disliked living with her grandmother and being separated from her parents.

At fifteen, Kimiko and her sister returned to BC. They attended school, but also had to look after their younger siblings (who were born while the two girls were in Japan) while her parents fished. Kimiko experienced intense culture shock. She had also lost most of the English she had learned as a girl. So, she got an English dictionary and taught herself to speak English again. One of her school teachers was the daughter of Mary Gyves (see page 38).

Kimiko's family's fishing business was successful, but they eventually sold the boats and bought farmland on Sharp Road, near Ganges Harbour and its famous farmers' market on northern Salt Spring Island. Kimiko's father built Salt Spring Island's first greenhouse and grew tomatoes in it. The family also grew an abundance of high-quality vegetables and berries.

In 1923 Kimiko became the first woman to drive on Salt Spring Island. She drove her Ford Model T truck to pick up chicken feed and sell eggs to Mouat's Store. The Okanos' produce was exceptional and was sold to high-end Victoria buyers like the Empress Hotel.

When Kimiko returned to Japan in 1925 for her grandmother's funeral, she met and married Katsuyori Murakami. They spent a few years in Japan and then returned to Canada together in 1932, buying their own farm on Salt Spring Island's Sharp Road and developing a successful market business selling their produce. They also had five children.

Everything changed when Japan bombed Pearl Harbour on December 1, 1941. Overnight, Japanese Canadians were viewed as "enemy aliens" and a security risk to Canada. They were distrusted and discriminated against. They faced daily harassment and racially motivated attacks. The seventy-seven Japanese-Canadian families on Salt Spring Island suddenly found themselves discriminated against based on their race.

On February 26, 1942, the Canadian government took action under the *War Measures Act*. This barred Japanese Canadians from a 161-kilometre area along the west coast of Canada. It also gave government officials the power to seize assets and intern all Canadian residents of Japanese descent. Many of these Japanese Canadians were born in Canada. As a result, 22,000 Japanese Canadians who lived in BC were sent to internment camps east of the Rocky Mountains. Kimiko's husband Katsuyori was taken away by government officials called the Custodians of Enemy Property. Soon after, a ship arrived to take away all Japanese Canadians living on Salt Spring Island, including Kimiko and her five children, who were aged between one and thirteen at the time. Kimiko had no idea where Katsuyori had been taken. They wouldn't be reunited until months later. Kimiko and the children grabbed what they could carry from their house and boarded the ship. The ship stopped at Mayne Island to pick up Japanese Canadians living there and then everyone on board was taken to Hastings Camp in Vancouver.

Kimiko Murakami

Kimiko Okano's passport photo. COURTESY OF THE SALT SPRING
ISLAND HISTORICAL SOCIETY ARCHIVES—MURAKAMI COLLECTION

Hastings Camp was an internment camp at the site of the
current Pacific National Exhibition and Playland. Back then, the
animal barracks were used to house the Japanese Canadians who
had been taken from their homes. The camp was bitter cold with
no indoor toilets or water. Eventually Kimiko and her children
were taken by train to an internment camp in the town of Green-
wood, in the Interior region of BC. Here too, living conditions were
abysmal. Kimiko and her children shared one filthy cubicle in a
crowded bunkhouse.

Later, Kimiko and her children were moved to Magrath,
Alberta, where they were forced to work at a sugar beet farm. They

were briefly moved to a different internment camp in the Slocan and then back to Magrath, Alberta. Living conditions were dismal in all the camps. They lived in unheated tents or shacks and were treated like criminals.

In 1944 Japanese Canadians were given the choice to return to Japan or continue working on the beet farm. The Murakamis stayed, holding out hope that, one day, they could return to their Salt Spring Island farm.

Four years after the war ended, Japanese Canadians were once again allowed to move, vote, and access the full rights they were entitled to as Canadian citizens. However, much damage had been done. Many Japanese Canadians had returned to Japan. Most settled elsewhere in Canada, with very few returning to BC. Many Canadians had a skewed and flawed view of Japanese Canadians after the war.

Kimiko's family ran a restaurant in Cardston, Alberta, until they had saved enough money to return to their old life. On Kimiko's fiftieth birthday, in 1954, Kimiko, Katsuyori, and their children returned to Salt Spring Island. They were the only Japanese-Canadian family to return there. Their land was gone, sold by the Canadian government without their consent. Any extra money from the sales of their assets was used to pay their internment fees. Many other families had the same experience.

Not only were they not welcomed, but Kimiko and her family faced blind hatred and racism. Their neighbours had turned on them. The banks harassed them. People vandalized their property. They suffered threats. They faced racism from businesses, the police, and the Anglican Church, which Kimiko had been baptized into.

Kimiko Murakami

The Murakamis didn't give up; instead, they began rebuilding their lives. They bought scrubland on Rainbow Road and built a farm business all over again. New buildings were put up and new farmland was cleared. Again, Kimiko's family worked hard at farming and growing high-quality vegetables and berries. The family's produce was still of the highest quality, and they had many employees working for them. In addition, the Japanese cemetery on Salt Spring Island had been used as a dump in the years they were gone and the family set to work cleaning it when they weren't farming. They also fixed grave markers that had been removed or vandalized. Eventually some people began changing their attitudes and saw the Murakamis for what they were: honest, hard-working, and community-minded.

KATSUYORI PASSED AWAY in 1988. In July of 1997, Kimiko passed away at Lady Minto Hospital on Salt Spring Island. She was sixty-six years old and was buried in Ganges Central Cemetery. Two hundred and fifty Salt Spring Island residents showed up for a community celebration in her honour.

A framed photo of Kimiko hangs on the wall of the National Archives of Canada in Ottawa. She is featured in a book written by her daughter Rose Murakami called *Ganbaru: The Murakami Family of Salt Spring Island*. Kimiko's face is featured on the hundred-dollar bill of Salt Spring dollars—legal tender on par with the Canadian dollar and only usable on Salt Spring Island. This made her the first person of Asian descent to be featured on legal tender anywhere in North America.

After Katsuyori and Kimiko passed away, racism continued to affect the Murakamis. Rose had graduated at the top of her class from UBC but was not allowed to be a nurse at Salt Spring Island's Lady Minto Hospital because of her ethnicity. She eventually earned two graduate degrees and became the Vice-President of Nursing at UBC's Health Sciences Centre.

In 2007 Rose and her brother Richard initiated a project to honour their parents: a supportive housing project that would offer safe and affordable housing to vulnerable families on Salt Spring Island. Murakami Gardens was a $4.9 million development supported by all three levels of government, Salt Spring Island Community Services, the Real Estate Foundation of BC, and the Murakami Family. Rose and Richard donated half an acre of land, valued at $1.2 million, to the project. Murakami Gardens opened in 2008, the first low-income housing project of its kind on Salt Spring Island.

Kimiko's daughter Rose remembered the conditions at the internship camps and told BC Housing, "We know what it's like to live in degrading and dehumanizing situations. We lived in some terrible, terrible places, you wouldn't even call them houses... We know what these individuals and families are going through. It is only through the support of the community that we can attempt to house and care for individuals in our community."

Kimiko was tremendously resilient. She is remembered as having a magnetic personality and never giving up. She thrived despite ongoing injustices. She had endured human rights atrocities and filthy internment camps, but she retained pride, hope, and integrity. She rebuilt her life on Salt Spring Island after everything was taken from her. She refused to become bitter and hateful. Kimiko never gave up, always did her best, and held on, embodying the true meaning of the word *ganbaru*.

8

Josephine Tilden
Marine Biologist and
Seaside Research Station Founder

JOSEPHINE TILDEN LIVED a relatively normal life until she became enchanted by the tide pools of a remote Vancouver Island beach after a rowing adventure through wild seas.

The year was 1900, and twenty-nine-year-old Josephine Tilden had travelled to Seattle from Minnesota by train, and from there to Victoria, BC, by boat; she then transferred to a steamship to take her the final hundred kilometres up the coast to a settlement now known as Port Renfrew. Today, Port Renfrew is famous as the launching point for the famous West Coast Trail hike. But back then, it was a remote wilderness settlement, far from civilization. A pioneer named Tom Baird had canoed with Josephine until they reached the shelf beach where a collection of remarkable tide pools lay.

Josephine Tilden holding her cat. UNIVERSITY OF MINNESOTA
ARCHIVES, UNIVERSITY OF MINNESOTA–TWIN CITIES

Josephine stayed on that remote beach for four days, following her passion, the reason she had come in the first place: Pacific algae. As a phycologist (scientist who studies algae), Josephine was in her element, exploring the natural aquariums created from boulders grinding out holes in the soft sandstone. The beach is now known as Botanical Beach in Juan De Fuca Provincial Park. Although thousands of people explore the tide pools every year, few know of Josephine Tilden and her amazing life.

AFTER THIS WEST coast journey Josephine's life changed. She wanted to set up a seaside research station for students of the University of Minnesota, where she was a professor. To make her dream a reality, she first needed approval from the university. They agreed to provide instructors and equipment, but the rest of the planning and expenses were up to Josephine. The rest turned out to be a lot.

For one thing, she needed to secure land. Thomas Baird, the man who had rowed with her on her first visit, owned a lot of land, likely under a pre-emption process where settlers were allotted large amounts of land with the promise that they will farm it. Josephine acquired a land deed for four acres along the ocean. Baird and some other locals built three buildings that would make up the seaside research station—a two-storey log cabin that served as living quarters for professors and students, a two-storey laboratory building, and a small laboratory building near the ocean. Since the University of Minnesota was only providing instructors and equipment, the costs of the land and building were Josephine's responsibility. She put her own money into the land, but needed help. The head of the department of botany at the university, Conway MacMillan, also contributed. The only other funding came from the students, who paid fees to study at the Minnesota Seaside Station when it officially opened in 1901.

Getting to the Minnesota Seaside Research Station was an adventure unto itself. Most students travelled from the landlocked states of Minnesota, Ohio, and Nebraska. They took a train to Seattle, often cooking in the rail cars, and then travelled by boat to Victoria and then by steamship to the nearly uninhabited village of Port Renfrew. The last leg of the journey was a several-kilometre hike, with the students carrying all their luggage, through mud and thick rainforest to arrive at the seaside research station, their home for the next month.

JOSEPHINE ELIZABETH TILDEN was born in Davenport, Iowa, in 1869. She attended the University of Minnesota, earning an undergraduate degree in 1895 and a master's degree in 1896. Soon after, she joined the university's faculty and, despite not having a doctorate degree, was soon promoted to full professor. She was the university's first female scientist and later became an internationally recognized authority on algae and on algal stalactites—icicle-like deposits found around thermal springs.

Between 1901 and 1907, the Seaside Station housed both professors and students. Life at the research station could be compared to a hybrid of a university field camp and an academic summer camp. Mornings consisted of botany lectures on the beach and outdoor lectures about zoology, taxonomy, or geology. Afternoons were spent collecting samples of algae and preserving them. After dinner, there might be an informal evening lecture or some fun: plays and bonfires, complete with mussels and saltwater toffee, were had along the beach. At the end of the day, tired students fell asleep to the sound of the waves, either in the cabin's sleeping quarters or on a mattress of evergreen boughs in driftwood beach shelters they had built themselves.

Women made up a large percentage of students at the seaside research station, as botany was a popular field of study for women in those days. Outdoor wear was not common for women in the 1900s, though, so they had to improvise. Some wore "short skirts" that sat about thirty centimetres above the ground. Under this skirt, the women wore bathing suits with high necks and long sleeves. This kept them warm when they got wet while collecting and preserving samples of algae. Others wore men's overalls. Most wore bicycle shoes with hobnails—boots with nails in the sole to provide grip on muddy and rough surfaces, like the cork boots worn by modern-day loggers, miners, and tree planters.

A station yearbook, called *Postelsia* (also the name of sea palm algae), not only documented the research done at the research station but also contained photographs of the beach bonfires, costumes, and plays. Other yearbook photos show women in long dresses clambering along the rocks, looking totally in their element on the wild west coast shoreline, or crouched over the large tide pools with nets, engrossed in their research and absolutely in the present.

In 1907 the University of Minnesota pulled the instructors and equipment, and cancelled all involvement with the Minnesota Seaside Research Station. They cited difficult access as one reason for their decision. Josephine and Conway MacMillan tried desperately to save the station, contributing even more of their own money. In a final report about the seaside station, Conway said they "bravely tried to carry on." In the end, it seemed the university administration and governing board did not value the station's work and insisted the university stop providing instructors. Conway left the research station in 1906, resigning his position at the university altogether, but Josephine kept going until 1907. With sadness and a sense of defeat, but also knowing she had done all she could to keep it going, Josephine finally admitted to herself it was impossible to keep the station afloat.

Josephine continued working at the University of Minnesota as a professor for the rest of her career, although she nurtured a lifelong grudge against the university over the closing of the Seaside Station. But even though her Seaside Station adventure was over, Josephine continued to have adventures elsewhere. She led numerous research expeditions comprising many female students to Tahiti, Australia, Tasmania, Hawaii, and New Zealand. In 1934, aged sixty-nine, she led a research expedition of ten students to the South Pacific to collect samples.

JOSEPHINE RETIRED IN 1937, after twenty-seven years of working for the university. She took her extensive algae collection with her and continued her research during retirement. In 1948 she sold her Port Renfrew property that had once housed the Minnesota Seaside Station. Josephine moved to Lake Wales, in central Florida, where she founded the Golden Bough Community for retired academics. She died in 1957, and a genus of moth, *Tildenia*, was named in her honour. Her scholarly accomplishments include three published books, fifty scientific articles, a bibliographic card file on the algae of the world, and the first American textbook on phycology. Josephine studied not only the algae found at the ocean, but also the blue-green algae (also called cyanobacteria) that occurs in the hot springs and geysers of Yellowstone National Park.

Many aspects of the sea lure us: its salty smell, its unpredictability, its mystery gifts while beachcombing. Tide pools are a microcosm for the magic of the entire ocean. There's something otherworldly about peering into tide pools, like peering into another universe. And they bring the oddities of the ocean within our reach. Crouching down and peering into the opening in the rocks reawakens a child-like sense of wonder even in the most adult of adults.

Josephine Tilden felt the lure of the sea. She not only soaked it up for her own enjoyment, but also built a place where others could explore its wonders for themselves. She was not only a conveyer of sea knowledge, but also a creator of sea knowledge—and she inspired many women to become botanists. I think she would be happy to know that university students are still drawn to the seaside and still explore and learn at the rugged shoreline and productive tide pools that she was drawn to and loved so deeply.

9

Dorothy Blackmore
Master Mariner
and Marine Engineer

DOROTHY BLACKMORE SQUEEZED her boat through the narrow mouth of the inlet where the loggers were stranded. She expertly navigated through a gale force wind and fierce waves before reaching the point of land where the two men awaited rescue. They were loggers on a timber-cruising and oyster-harvesting trip gone wrong. Their boat had crashed into a log, leaving them stranded for two days and one night with only oysters to eat. When the police got the call, they contacted Dorothy Blackmore. She was credited for the rescue and later received a letter of thanks signed by Julius Bloedel, owner of the prominent Canadian forestry company the two rescued men worked for: Bloedel, Stewart and Welch.

DOROTHY CLARICE BLACKMORE was born in Port Alberni, BC, in 1914. Her father, George Blackmore, owned Blackmore Marine

Services, primarily a water taxi service. Dorothy's older brother had no interest in boats, so George taught Dorothy the family business. At ten years old, she was driving boats solo.

After finishing high school, Dorothy started driving boats full-time. She drove fast, and she drove well. Speed was essential in the boating business, as the first boat there got the job. She qualified for her Master Ship Captain papers at twenty-one years old but could not get certified. It was 1935, and many industries still did not consider women to be "persons," no matter what the law said.

Dorothy's father advocated on her behalf. He pressured A.W. Neill, Port Alberni's Member of Parliament at the time, to get federal legislation changed to allow women to earn their captain papers. A pilot, who she drove around for work, also rallied to her cause, pressuring the Department of Transportation to honour the Lord Chancellor's 1929 ruling that stated women were in fact persons. The lobbying worked. A letter to Dorothy's father, on House of Commons letterhead and signed "A.W. Neill," stated: "I am advised that the Department has decided that a woman is eligible to receive a certificate as master, mate or engineer, if she fulfils all the requirements of the *Canada Shipping Act*, so I trust that this will lead to your daughter getting the certificate she desires." The words "has earned" seem more accurate than "desires," considering she rightfully met the requirements for the certificate.

Twenty-three-year-old Dorothy, the first female sea captain in Canada, had made history. She featured in newspaper headlines in Montreal, Vancouver, Seattle, and Alabama, described in terms such as "Coast Girl Picks Life on Tugboat" and "Madame Captain." Photos below the headlines show Dorothy in her marine coveralls, with a smile as big as a modern-day lottery winner, speeding

Dorothy Blackmore in captain hat. PATRICIA AND BOB CURRIE

through the water holding a boat's steering wheel. A cartoon of Dorothy was even featured on Sweet Marie chocolate bars.

One article talks about her "invading" traditional male domains, despite being presented as a congratulatory piece. Another condescendingly joked about her marrying the first mate, having an all-female crew so she wouldn't have to delegate to men, and having a husband in every port. Others focused largely on her youth and attractive looks, rather than her competence and achievements.

Dorothy worked as a master ship captain from 1924 to 1957. She taxied loggers from Port Alberni to logging camps, drove air force personnel to air force stations during the Second World War, and helped incoming freighters with docking lines. Much work was done in the *Commodore III*—a twenty-eight-foot, thirty knot, twin-engine speedboat. Along with becoming the first female

Master Sea Captain in Canada, Dorothy became a 3rd class engineer in 1940.

Dorothy drove boats over waters that were volatile and unpredictable. Kind, turquoise water that begged to be driven fast over. Dense, dark waters that kicked up vicious storms, especially in winter. Waters that earned a reputation as "the Graveyard of the Pacific" after banishing many hundreds of souls to watery graves.

The Second World War affected not only Dorothy's marine career but also her personal life. She was a member of the Merchant Marine, which was highly unusual for a woman at that time, and as a captain in open waters, she frequently drove air force personnel to stations in Ucluelet and Tofino. She was offered an Order of the British Empire (OBE) for her work on the west coast during the war, but turned it down. During the war she became engaged to a captain, but broke it off. Around this time her father fell ill and couldn't work, so Dorothy ran Blackmore Marine Services on her own.

After the war Dorothy married a Royal Canadian Air Force squadron leader named Pitt Clayton. When her father eventually sold his boats, Dorothy worked with Pitt driving sport fishing boats for a company they named Port Boat House (which still exists today). They bought eighty acres in Nanoose Bay and started Clayton's Fishing Resort as a second business in the fishing off-season. Once Clayton's Fishing Resort was well established, they sold Port Boat House. After their two daughters were born, Dorothy took some time off from driving boats, but eventually the ocean called her back. She reactivated her boating certifications, which had expired, and in the 1950s drove tugboats for Island Tug and Barge, all while she and Pitt kept Clayton Fishing Resort going. Things had changed since she had last driven boats. Marine radios, to communicate with other captains about tides and weather, made being a captain much easier than Dorothy remembered.

Dorothy loved her work. She didn't mind being on call twenty-four hours a day and heading out by boat when a freighter arrived during off-hours. An article in *Pacific Boat Motor* in 1945 quotes her as saying she would "go crazy if she had to teach or work in a bank, like her sisters." In an interview with the CBC, Dorothy's daughter Patricia Currie talked about her mom's friendly rivalry with the captain of the *Uchuck*, the famous converted minesweeper freighter. He and Dorothy both got a call about a boat needed to drive someone in Ucluelet to hospital. They raced to get there first. The *Uchuck* captain turned around due to bad weather; Dorothy got the patient safely to hospital. Dorothy was casual about her accomplishments, apparently never thinking what she did was extraordinary. To her, driving boats fast was just another day at work.

Eventually, Dorothy and Pitt sold Clayton's Fishing Resort, but they did not abandon the world of boats in their retirement. They moved to England and bought a sailboat, which they sailed mostly around the Mediterranean before selling it. A few years later they returned to Canada and bought another boat, which they also sold—and then bought a third sailboat, in which they cruised many of the rivers in Europe.

DOROTHY DIED IN Grand Forks, BC, in 1996, at the age of eighty-two. She had been a true trailblazer. She made history at only twenty-three years old by becoming the first female ship captain in Canada. She had a zest for life and excelled in a male-dominated career. She showed courage, skill, and dedication to her boating career.

10

Emma Stark
Pioneer and Teacher

SALT SPRING ISLAND, the traditional territory of the Cowichan Coast Salish peoples, rests in the Salish Sea, north of Victoria and south of Nanaimo. Today it is known for its tranquil beaches, lively harbours, hip shops, charming roadside farm stands, and established farmers markets brimming with artisans and farmers. In the mid-nineteenth century, it was a place of untouched forest, green hills, lakes, and valleys perfect for farming. Immigrants from Hawaii, Japan, and Europe eventually settled there, but the first settlers were from California.

IN 1860 SYLVIA and Louis Stark, African Americans from California, arrived on Salt Spring Island in search of freedom, land, and a life free of discrimination. Former slaves from Missouri and Kentucky respectively, they had met in California. When legal and educational limitations began affecting their freedoms, it was time to move again. They were not prepared to lose the freedom they had worked so hard to achieve.

James Douglas, Vancouver Island's Governor at the time, invited hundreds of African Americans from California to settle on Vancouver Island and the surrounding Gulf Islands. Concerned about American incursions, he wanted to increase the Canadian population. In 1858 eight hundred African Americans arrived on the Saanich peninsula. From there, they spread out to various locations on Vancouver Island and the Gulf Islands. Two or three dozen of them went to Salt Spring Island. Sylvia and Louis Stark arrived in 1860.

Sylvia's father, Howard Estes, was born a slave in Clay County, Missouri. In 1852 he bought his and his family's freedom for $4,000. Sylvia was living in Placerville, California, when she met Louis Stark, who was dairy farming at the time. Louis had been born into slavery on a plantation in Louisville, Kentucky, and at some point bought his freedom for $1,500. Sylvia and Louis were married in California and had their first two children, Willis and Serena, there.

To get to Salt Spring Island, Sylvia and Louis sailed on the *Black Diamond* from Saanich to Salt Spring Island. As was customary back then, the schooner dropped them off a way from shore and they swam ashore with their belongings and livestock.

Two hundred acres of Salt Spring Island mountainside wilderness was their very own. So were freedom, equality, and a life free of discrimination. Pioneer life was not easy. But they were free. The oath of allegiance they took upon arriving in Canada gave them the rights and privileges of British subjects. Their acreage was located near Vesuvius Bay, and the family immediately set to work felling trees to build a house, barn, and fences. Sylvia and Louis also had three more children, one of whom they named Emma Arabella Stark.

After two of their fellow immigrants on Salt Spring Island were murdered, Louis and Sylvia feared for their family's safety. One of the men had been the family's hired help and the other was a Sunday school teacher. Louis requested his pre-emption land rights be transferred to the coal mining town of Nanaimo, and the family moved to a 365-acre property in the Cranberry area of Nanaimo, next to the current day Chase River Elementary School. Louis planted many apple and other fruit trees on their new farm.

The Starks valued education and at some point sent Emma and her sister Marie to North Cedar School as there was no school in the Cranberry area. Back then, it was common for students who lived far from the school to live in a cabin beside the school during the week. Emma and Marie did this, since their house was more than thirteen kilometres away. Sylvia would come and get the girls to bring them home at weekends. They travelled by horseback, Marie riding with their mother and Emma riding her own horse. When the bridge over the Cedar River was being repaired, Emma would likely have ridden through water so deep that her legs would have been submerged in the cold river water. In winter, they travelled in a hand-built oxen-pulled sled.

Sylvia missed the quiet and her community on Salt Spring Island; their Chase River property's proximity to coal mines had caused it to shake and vibrate constantly. After some time in Nanaimo, she returned to Salt Spring Island, moving to a farm where her son Willis lived. Emma and her father remained in Nanaimo.

Emma Stark

Emma (Emily Arabella) Stark. SALT SPRING ISLAND HISTORICAL
SOCIETY ARCHIVES–ESTES/ STARK COLLECTION

In 1895, when Emma was eleven years old, tragedy struck the
Stark family. Late one night, Louis Stark was found dead at the
bottom of a cliff near the family's farm. Their neighbour, a butcher,
told police that Louis had been hunting when he last saw him.

Louis' death was mysterious. Foul play was suspected, and the
butcher was the prime suspect. The motive was thought to concern the Starks' land, which contained large amounts of coal.

A prominent family of Nanaimo coal miners had apparently approached Louis, asking to buy the land, but Louis refused to sell. His reason: he had worked too hard farming it to sell.

An investigation was launched, a trial was conducted—and nobody was charged. Some think the butcher was hired by the Nanaimo coal mining family who wanted to mine Stark's land. Some say the mining family paid the butcher $50 to commit the murder and, when found not guilty, the butcher left for England with his money. Louis Stark was buried in the Nanaimo Municipal Cemetery on Bowen Road; a large headstone remains today bearing his name.

Despite her father's tragic death, Emma finished high school and became a teacher. At that time, a high school diploma was the only qualification a teacher needed. On August 1, 1874, eighteen-year-old Emma became the first African-American school teacher on all of Vancouver Island when she was hired to teach at the new Cedar-Cranberry school, a one-room schoolhouse that students travelled far distances to attend. She taught there until 1879, earning $40 a month, and was said to be a competent teacher who was well liked by students. She lived with her sister Marie in a small cabin by the school, as it wasn't practical for her to travel more than thirteen kilometres each way to her family property in Chase River, Nanaimo.

In 1878 Emma married James Clark in Victoria. From her marriage to her death, little is known of her life. She died young, aged only thirty-three, and her cause of death is unknown. She was buried in Salt Spring Island next to her grandfather, Howard Estes. Emma's mom, Sylvia, later became a prominent personality on Salt

Spring Island. Depending on which source you consult, she lived to be 105, more or less making her the oldest person on the island at the time of her death.

EMMA'S STORY IS one of freedom and self-determination. After her family made a long journey to freedom, Emma not only endured the many hardships so typical of pioneer life, but also became educated and passed on the gift of knowledge to her young students. Emma was welcomed into the community and did not seem to experience the discrimination that the family had faced before moving to Canada.

The Stark farm is now a heritage property in Nanaimo. At time of writing, the barn still stands, on Extension Road, beside Chase River Elementary School. Stark Lake, in the Extension area of Nanaimo, and Stark Landing, where the railroad passed the Stark family orchard and cattle fields, are named after the family. In the quaint Old City section of Nanaimo's downtown at 331 Wesley Street, where she once lived, a plaque bears Emma Stark's name. Put there in 1999, during the City of Nanaimo's 125th anniversary, it honours her as "the first Black teacher on Vancouver Island."

11

Aloha Wanderwell
Driver and Photographer

"BRAINS, BEAUTY AND Breeches—World Tour Offer for Lucky Young Woman... Wanted to Join an Expedition." So read the advertisement in the Paris newspaper. The restless and bold sixteen-year-old English schoolgirl couldn't resist. She applied.

The advertisement was for a filmmaker and secretary for a seven-year adventure around the world. The man advertising the position was Walter Wanderwell. Originally called Valerian Johannes Pieczynski, he was a former sailor, hiker, avid adventurer, and referred to as "Captain." In 1919 Walter and his wife Nell started Wanderwell Expeditions, a round-the-world endurance race with competing teams trying to log the most miles in their 1917 Ford Model Ts. In 1922 he and Nell separated, and he sought a new filmmaker, driver, and secretary.

The schoolgirl who responded to the advertisement spoke French, German, and some Italian. After the tour she would speak some Japanese and Russian also. She was fit, strong, and six feet tall. Her mother gave her permission to join the tour on the condition that she change her name for it to safeguard the family name. And so, Aloha Wanderwell came to be. Could there be a more fitting name for an adventurer than that?

Virtually unknown, but utterly worthy of knowing, Aloha proved to be the ultimate adventurer. In 1922, still aged sixteen, she began the trip that would make her the first woman to drive around the world. When most young women her age were preparing for marriage and settling into domestic roles, she was speeding around the world—driving, flying, and developing photographs. She's been called the world's most travelled woman, a female Indiana Jones, and the Amelia Earhart of the automobile.

ALOHA WAS BORN Idris Galcia Hall in 1906 in Winnipeg, Manitoba. Her family moved to North Vancouver, Victoria, Duncan, and then Qualicum Beach. Her childhood was spent in Qualicum Beach, where her family had a large amount of waterfront land that later became Judges Row and is currently filled with beach houses. Hall Road in Qualicum Beach is named after Aloha's family.

In 1917 Aloha's father died in the Battle of Ypres, and her mother subsequently moved the family to Europe. Aloha attended a convent boarding school in Nice, France. The school bored and stifled Aloha. She was smart as a whip, restless, and adventurous. She read adventure books that had been her father's, hid romance novels under her mattress (sneaked in by the convent housekeepers for her), and was repeatedly disciplined for opening her dormitory windows. She yearned to gaze at the ocean, see roads, and smell the fresh air. On her fourth visit to the principal's office over open windows, the school gave in and allowed Aloha special open window permissions.

Aloha was born for adventure, and her adventure of a lifetime began with her acceptance into the round-the-world driving tour. Finally, she could live authentically. She wore beige riding breeches, a white shirt, goggles, and a flying helmet. She was living her dream life, but she didn't forget her family—she sent her wages home to her mother and sister.

By day, Walter, Aloha, and their crew drove and filmed, with Aloha and Walter driving in separate Model Ts. By night they developed and edited the day's footage. The documentaries they made, what were then called "travel lectures," showed the amazing places they travelled through, and the lecture screenings funded their trip. They played the movies to audiences in every city they stopped in. Audiences were enthralled by the footage. It's easy to forget how difficult it was to access information in the pre-Internet era.

Upon joining the tour, Aloha travelled fourth-class on a ship from Marseilles, France, to Port Said, Egypt. The ticket manager nearly did not allow her onto the ship as a fourth-class passenger, because she was a young woman. Aloha insisted she be let aboard, explaining she had a job waiting for her and that her ticket was her way to make more money. The manager let her aboard. Fourth-class conditions were filthy and crowded. Her sleeping cot was among French soldiers, and on her first night she kicked one in the face when he tried to assault her. The other soldiers beat him up, put him in chains, and put tarps around Aloha's cot for privacy. She camped in a tent on the back of the sphinx in Egypt. She walked through Cairo's red-light district and witnessed funeral pyres in India. She was the first woman to drive from Bombay to

Aloha Wanderwell and Miki Hall. RICHARD DIAMOND AND
WWW.ALOHAWANDERWELL.COM

Calcutta. In India, a raja tried gifting her an elephant, but she graciously turned it down. He then tried giving her a camel, which she also politely declined. Undaunted, he then offered Aloha a monkey, which she accepted and named Chango. Every good adventure should have a monkey.

While at a masquerade ball in Calcutta, India, Aloha had her most dangerous experience of her travels. She got a mosquito bite that became seriously infected. She eventually saw a doctor who was paid a quart of quality whisky to lance the bite and treat the infection. Aloha had travelled unscathed through areas embroiled in civil wars of the time, escaped the threat of death squads in China, diplomatically spurned advances by powerful, often dangerous men—and then nearly died from the bite of a tiny mosquito.

Aloha and Walter not only fell in love on the tour, they married in California during it. Marriage did not slow Aloha down or tempt her into a life of domesticity. She ate coconut and lychee fruit picked from the roadside near Singapore. In the United States, she was arrested and charged $200 for impersonating an army officer after her outfit was mistaken for an army uniform. She hunted crocodiles, braved storms on a freighter from the US to Africa, camped near lions and jackals, and was made an honorary colonel of the Red Army of Siberia. Aloha and Walter edited their footage in a real film studio in Kyoto, Japan. Before she was twenty, Aloha had visited places many men and women never visit over the course of a lifetime. Her passport had more stamps than the passports of many avid modern-day travellers.

Aloha's sister Margaret Hall, whom the family called Miki, was also an amazing woman. She had been at the same convent boarding school in France as Aloha. The girls' mother told Miki to go along on the tour as a chaperone, so Miki joined the tour for several stints between 1924 and 1929. She was present for the Cape-to-Cairo leg of the journey, which was one of the journey's most gruelling sections.

The expedition finished in 1927, and in 1932, Walter and Aloha bought a yacht called the *Carma*, which they planned to sail while they continued making films. That plan was crushed when Walter was fatally shot on the yacht in Long Beach, California. The main suspect was found not guilty. No one has ever been charged with his death.

In 1933 Aloha married Walter Baker, one of Walter Wanderwell's former cameramen, whom she met while in Wyoming. The couple travelled, explored, and made documentaries from 1933 until 1942.

Aloha Wanderwell

ALOHA WAS REBELLIOUS but also wholesome. She was open to adventure and did whatever it took to get her car through myriad countries. She refused to drink, smoke, or swear. She loved driving steep, treacherous roads. But she also loved lavish hotel rooms and hot baths.

In 1939, when she was thirty-three, Aloha wrote a memoir based on her detailed trip journals. She titled it *Call to Adventure*. It chronicles her seven-year, round-the-world expedition through eighty countries and makes clear that she craved adventure and thrived on novelty. New food, new cultures, new people, and new experiences. She was most at home in new and exciting places.

Her retirement years involved preserving artifacts and films from her many adventures. She and Walter Baker lived on Lido Island, a manmade island near Newport Beach, California. Miki lived on Vancouver Island, in a house in Merville built by Walter that she named Windsong. She spent her summers there and winters on Lido Island with Aloha and Walter.

Aloha passed away in 1996 in Newport Beach, California, a year after Walter, and also a year after Miki had passed in Comox, BC.

Aloha Wanderwell had a fulsome career. Her varied jobs included cinematographer, driver, director, documentary maker, writer, and photographer. She was also a lecturer in travel at the National History Museum in Los Angeles. Adventure was the theme of her life. She chased adventure from the moment she was old enough to make her own decisions, and made it into the *Guinness Book of World Records* as the first woman to drive around the world. Aloha was a brave woman who lived life authentically, valuing adventure and travel over other more traditional roles.

12

Ada Annie Rae-Arthur
Backcountry Entrepreneur, Gardener, and Bounty Hunter

TO VISIT COUGAR Annie's garden, you must journey far past Tofino. In the 1900s, when Cougar Annie was living there, Tofino was well off the beaten path. It required a lengthy logging-road drive across Vancouver Island, followed by a ride on a motor boat through offshore reefs, kelp beds, rafts of sea otters, and exposed ocean. If the sea was calm, after a few hours of boating you would pass a cove with pools of hot water and hotter waterfalls, eventually flowing into the ocean. Finally, you would drop anchor just off an expansive beach at a place called Boat Basin.

You jump from the boat, your feet landing softly in white sand. The trail you walk passes through oversized trees that wear moss like thick green beards and long scraggly white-green hair. Tropical-looking ferns spring from the forest floor. Suddenly, the forest opens up and you're in a clearing. A garden. You see a tiny woman of 1.6 metres, wearing black gum boots and a faded floral dress. She's kneeling, hands in the dirt, tending to some extravagant, white dahlia flowers. A shotgun rests on the ground beside her. She looks up and you make eye contact. Meet Cougar Annie.

COUGAR ANNIE IS a full-on west coast legend. Perhaps because she lived the Vancouver Island dream—homesteading, living off the land, being her own boss, growing her own food, and living life her own way—when these things were survival necessities, not hip and trendy life goals. Maybe you've heard of her or you know parts of her story.

Cougar Annie started life as Ada Annie Jordan, born in Sacramento, California, in 1888. She arrived in Boat Basin as Ada Annie Rae-Arthur in 1915. Her parents were both from England, and the family had moved around (living in South Africa, Lloydminster, and Winnipeg) before settling in Vancouver when Ada Annie was in her late teens. Ada Annie was living in Vancouver and working at her father's veterinary clinic when she met Willie Rae-Arthur, a man from Glasgow, Scotland. The couple was married in 1909, and when Willie developed an opium addiction, Annie decided that moving to a west coast peninsula, far from the opium dens of Vancouver, was just the fresh start they needed. Annie, Willie, their three children, and their cow arrived by steamship in Hesquiat, a small Indigenous community located between Tofino and Gold River. From there, they paddled a dugout canoe to Boat Basin, where a cabin and 117 acres of raw land awaited them.

This land was theirs under the land pre-emption process, which encouraged agricultural development by giving settlers a generous amount of land at a good price to develop agriculturally. Transforming acres of thick, harsh, coastal rainforest into a homestead garden and various business ventures was gruelling work, but this was Cougar Annie's life. Whether or not she resented her husband for the situation, she certainly thrived through many adversities.

The brunt of the exhausting homesteading chores and responsibilities fell on Cougar Annie's shoulders, but she also found time to set traps and run a post office and store—all the while caring for children (she was pregnant through much of the first sixteen years at Boat Basin) and being wary of lurking cougars.

Willie, on the other hand, did not embrace the pioneer lifestyle. He preferred to read books, write poetry, nap, or boat to Tofino to drink and gamble.

Finances were an ongoing challenge, and Cougar Annie devised various ingenious ways of generating income, including opening a post office, store, and mail-order nursery and hunting cougars for bounty. Considering her remote location, Cougar Annie's business ventures were particularly inventive and impressive. Perhaps, she built on entrepreneurial skills learned in Vancouver, where she would bring in stray dogs through her back door, wash them, and sell them out her front door.

Shooting cougars was Cougar Annie's claim to fame. In *Cougar Annie's Garden*, Margaret Horsfield attributes Cougar Annie's sharp shooting ability to her father teaching her to shoot at seven years old. Shooting cougars served a dual purpose: to protect her goats (a valuable source of milk) and to make income through bounty payments. Some sources say Cougar Annie killed sixty-five cougars during her time at Boat Basin; others put the number at over eighty. Whatever the number, she was said to be a dead shot,

Ada Annie Rae-Arthur

Cougar Annie at Boat Basin. IMAGE C-04904 COURTESY OF BC MUSEUM AND ARCHIVES. PHOTO TAKEN BY JOHN MANNING.

earning her a rather epic reputation (and nickname) up and down the west coast of Vancouver Island.

The Boat Basin store opened around 1923, out of one of the four rooms in her house. Horsfield writes that Cougar Annie's store sold staples such as cigarettes, tobacco, sardines, chocolate bars, crackers, tinned food, matches, canned milk, sugar, butter, and yeast. Due to their alcoholic content, vanilla extract and lemon extract were the biggest sellers. Cougar Annie was a fickle store owner. Prices fluctuated wildly, and although rules on expiry dates hadn't yet been introduced, she pushed food safety to the limits by selling old and rotten chicken eggs. Horsfield tells of three people buying the same thing on the same day and being charged three different prices. Annie's customers included Hesquiat people, fishermen, missionaries, police, and lighthouse keepers, all of whom had no other choice of store.

In 1935 Cougar Annie applied for a Canada Post office at Boat Basin. The application required a petition which, according to Margaret Horsfield, had thirty-six signatures in suspiciously similar handwriting. The post office secured Annie a monthly salary and attracted customers from her store. It operated from 1936 until the mid-1980s.

Cougar Annie went to great lengths to keep the post office busy and ensure a consistent salary for herself. Horsfield says she often bought books of stamps to make it seem busy. She sent stamps as gifts, bartered with stamps (with Parksville's Buckerfield's feed store), pressured family and store customers to purchase stamps, and eventually discovered a use for her stamps that would also bring her immense joy—a nursery business.

A mail-order nursery business was a truly clever business idea. She had a post office. She had a garden. Why not combine both and have a business that maximized her love of gardening? Cougar Annie advertised her stock in farm magazines, received orders by mail, and shipped out orders via the coastal steamship that delivered mail and store supplies. She named her business Lawson's Bulb Garden (she had changed her name after a recent marriage). It kept the post office busy and gave her some precious interaction with the outside world. While her other ventures had put food on the table, Lawson's Bulb Garden satiated Cougar Annie's heart and soul. She delighted in ordering varied and unique plants from faraway places like Chile and Japan, and sold plants of all kinds: shrubs, mosses, ferns, fruit trees, and roses. But most popular were her dahlia bulbs. She received orders from across Canada and even Europe for her dahlias. Later in life, when she was nearly blind, she continued to take great care and even greater pride in wrapping dahlia bulbs in sphagnum moss before mailing them to customers. Sending and receiving personal notes from customers gave her a connection with the wider world and to people who shared her love of gardening. It also proved to be a source of comfort through life's inevitable griefs and losses.

Heartbreak and loss were constant throughout Cougar Annie's life. In a far back corner of the garden, white heather and stones mark a gravesite. Buried there are three of Cougar Annie's husbands, her teenage son who drowned, and three infants.

Margaret Horsfield discusses Cougar Annie's marriages in *Cougar Annie's Garden*. Willie Rae-Arthur drowned while rowing to collect mail from the *Princess Maquinna*, the ship that delivered passengers and freight up and down the coast. Although his work ethic had been deplorable, his passing meant all the tasks relating to running the homestead and businesses and raising the children now landed solely on Cougar Annie. She didn't let that stop her. She put an ad for a husband in two farm newspapers, the *Western Producer* and *Winnipeg Free Press*. The ad read: "BC widow with nursery and orchard wishes partner. Widower preferred. Object matrimony." This was searching for love before the Internet and online dating.

Without their ever having met in person, George Campbell was selected as her next spouse and arrived at Boat Basin in 1940, accompanied by a minister from Bamfield, who married them that same day. George died four years later of a gunshot wound to his groin. His death was gossiped about. Cougar Annie claimed he shot himself while cleaning his gun, but some think she shot him because he was abusive.

Once again, Cougar Annie placed an ad in farm magazines. This time, Esau Arnold, a farmer from Saskatchewan, was chosen.

He spent ten years in Boat Basin, until he passed away from pneumonia.

Robert Culvert, a poultry farmer from Salmon Arm, was the closest Cougar Annie came to finding kindred companionship in her mail-order husbands. His three children accompanied him to Boat Basin, and Horsfield describes him as being gentle, kind, loving, soft-spoken, hard-working, and handy. After fixing many fences and sharing a loving partnership, Robert left Boat Basin in poor health. Amicable letters were exchanged for years to come and the two remained friends for life. Years after his initial departure, he returned to Boat Basin for a few years, inventing a motor-ized wheelbarrow to bring supplies from the beach to the garden.

George Lawson was Cougar Annie's final husband. He arrived in 1960, and a coastal missionary married the couple. She was seventy-two years old; he was sixty. Seven years after arriving, George left. Some say Cougar Annie sent him away at gunpoint because of his drinking, stealing from the store, and abusive behaviour. Cougar Annie did not ever marry for love, but for help on the homestead. Her garden and homestead prevailed through her marriage's beginnings and ends.

The departure of her children was a different sort of loss. Except for her son Tommy Rae-Arthur, who helped her run the post office and cared for her, Cougar Annie's children all left Boat Basin as soon as possible. The boys sought employment up and down the coast and the girls landed in Victoria. This must have been hard on Cougar Annie. She left Boat Basin on only a handful of occasions over her long life—once after breaking her elbow. For much of her time at Boat Basin, coastal steamship from Victoria was her only way to access the outside world.

However, Cougar Annie was as hardy as her heather plants were prolific. In her seventies, she still tended to her chickens. At ninety-two years old, she still lived in her wood-heated homestead and drank rainwater from her roof. Nearly blind, she navigated around her garden by feeling fencepost to fencepost. She sleep-walked in her beloved garden. She was one tough woman.

Her garden was her life. Given the choice, Cougar Annie would have stayed in her garden forever. In 1983, however, her health deteriorated to the point where she had to move. In 1985 Cougar Annie passed away as Ada Annie Lawson in Port Alberni. She was ninety-six years old. Her ashes were scattered over her garden: truly the centre of her universe.

COUGAR ANNIE'S GARDEN still exists. A wilderness paradise and gem of natural history, it is mysterious and magical in a wild, secret-garden way. Up from the ocean, with rotting boards still present from her original paths, large trees shelter the garden from harsh sea winds. A wooden archway and boardwalk welcome you into the garden where you can see raised beds that once held dahlias and other flowers. Further along is an orchard with grapes and twenty-five types of heirloom apples that Cougar Annie likely planted from seed. A dilapidated house in the centre of the garden struggles to stand and keep alive the memory of Cougar Annie's house, post office, and store. A forest of mature rhododendrons brazenly outlines one side of the garden.

Cougar Annie's garden would have been devoured by the rainforest were it not for one person who came into her life. Peter Buckland first met Cougar Annie when he came to Boat Basin as a prospector in 1968. Over the following eighteen years he returned often to assist her. In 1981, at Annie's insistence, Peter purchased the property, moved to Boat Basin, and commenced what would become a thirty-one-year project to recover the garden from forty years of overgrowth. Annie continued to live there without running water or electricity.

In 1998 Peter created the Boat Basin Foundation as a charitable organization. Its objectives are to preserve the garden and to promote interest and education in natural history. The Foundation constructed the Temperate Rainforest Field Study Centre as a place where groups can stay on site and appreciate the surrounding natural history. The Foundation also offers day visits to visitors who seaplane into Boat Basin from Tofino.

Peter refers to Cougar Annie as Ada Annie. Endearingly. Like the old friend she was to him. The respect he has for her is tangible, and he talks of the deep responsibility he felt to maintain the precious piece of natural history she created. He helped Cougar Annie for many years, including in 1969 when she required cataract surgery and was elderly and living at Boat Basin. He has brought his own flair to the property, with numerous intricate wooden buildings and structures, including an eagle woodshed, boardwalks, lakeside buildings, and cabins. He has also ensured that Cougar Annie's legacy is preserved.

Cougar Annie wielded unwavering courage and overcame immense hardships in an isolated, unforgiving place. She carved out various income-generating businesses in a wet and wild place in which many people would struggle to simply survive. Although she is one of many determined pioneers, her story stands out. She might have been small in stature, but she has left a substantial legacy as a Canadian heroine.

13

Ann Elmore Haig-Brown
Librarian and Social Advocate

ANN HAIG-BROWN'S STORY is one bound by books and letters and set in a garden homestead called Above Tide. It is a story about two people beautifully suited to one other, and a relationship woven with accomplishments, both joint and individual. It's a story of courage, resilience, and advocacy for women and children.

MUCH OF WHAT we know about Ann and Roderick Haig-Brown comes from *Deep Currents*, a biography their daughter Valerie wrote. Ann Elmore was a city girl, born in Seattle. Her parents, a head operating room nurse and a doctor, met at work. Ann was a lover of books and nature from a young age. She achieved the highest possible scores in the University of Washington psychology department and went on to attend the University of California at Berkeley for a Bachelor of Arts degree.

Ann Elmore. IMAGE 20363-43 COURTESY
OF THE MUSEUM AT CAMPBELL RIVER

After university, Ann worked in a well-known bookstore where she introduced the people of Seattle to the best books of the day. She wrote reviews for the bookstore's monthly newsletter. One day, a tall, kind man sauntered into the bookstore. He too was a lover of books and nature. He and Ann connected immediately and began exchanging letters.

The man's name was Roderick Haig-Brown. Originally from England, he had come to Canada to work on northern Vancouver Island. He not only loved books, he was actually a writer. When they met, he was writing a book about cougars. He later told Ann that he fell in love with her intellect, her red hair, and her love of books.

Their letters, back and forth, were mostly about books—a shared passion and a matter impersonal enough to discuss early in a relationship with no risk of impropriety. They sent books to each other and later discussed them in-depth in letters. This continued for three years. During this time, they discussed marriage. The problem was lack of money. Roderick promised to propose when they had enough saved, and then saved so desperately that Ann wrote that she was worried he would starve himself by saving money so fiercely. When they eventually got engaged their letters contained discussions about wedding plans and designs for their house, garden, and married life.

Ann and Roderick both planned for married life. Roderick found a house to rent in Campbell River—a town at the end of the main road on Vancouver Island—and purchased a boat to allow them to explore the area by water. Ann, a very competent and speedy typist, bought a typewriter and a Ford for them to drive. In letters to her fiancé, Ann excitedly describes the light brown Ford coupe, with its space for two steamer trunks.

The couple married in Seattle on January 20, 1934. For their honeymoon, they drove south in the Ford coupe through California to Mexico.

Married life was a balance of blessed bliss and regular life obstacles. They made butter, cultivated bountiful gardens, lounged in front of a cozy fire savouring music, and enjoyed adventures such as camping on the spit in Campbell River or at Buttle Lake. They had three dogs, but their most unusual pet was the cougar kitten they adopted. One photo shows Ann walking it on leash through a field. Several of Roderick's writings featured the cougar kitten.

Life was generally good except for one thing: Ann was not pregnant. She was diagnosed with a displaced uterus and an adherent appendix, and a doctor friend of her father subsequently performed surgery. The surgery proved successful, and eventually Ann was pregnant with their first child, whom they named Valerie. The baby was born in Seattle, so Ann could be near her mother and sister.

Finances were a constant concern for the first few years for the couple. They lived off Roderick's writing and ate from their garden. Things became a little easier when Roderick's grandfather left the couple enough money that they could buy a house just up the river. They named it Above Tide. This would be their forever home and the launching pad for many adventures, several books, and four children. The gardens were a constant source of pride and delight to both of them—and supplied the family with fresh, healthy food, lessening grocery bills. Their bounty included squash, broccoli, corn, beans, peas, celery, cabbages, melons, peppers, and cucumbers. They didn't sell any of the food, but they ate well.

Life ebbed and flowed. The first year at Above Tide, their two black labs went missing. Roderick searched far and wide for them and found them across the river two weeks later, thin and cut up. One Sunday morning, an earthquake sent books flying off shelves, trees shaking in the yard, and a stove pipe falling in the indoor hearth. One summer, Ann took the children to Seattle because of the threat of forest fires approaching their house.

Money was still tight, but overall life was good. Valerie's account of life at Above Tide conjures up happy images straight from the pages of a glossy cottage magazine: Ann in her vegetable garden, Roderick milking the cows, the children playing with the dogs and making fishing rods from sticks. This dream was interrupted when Roddy left to fight in the Second World War. Until then, they had not been greatly affected by the war. Now, like so many couples, they would be apart.

With Roderick gone, Ann had to do the work of two people, maintaining the household and gardens, and raising the children, now aged seven, five, and eighteen months. She adjusted her life and got on with it. She got up earlier in the morning and the children helped with age-appropriate chores.

Ann and Roderick operated as a team even when apart. They stayed connected by writing once again. Roderick's letters told Ann about where he was. Her letters told of weeding the garden, beach days, and bedtime stories. They discussed how to fix the mower; finances, which were still tight despite his army pay; friends; neighbours; and picnics at the mouth of the Campbell River. And of course, their letters also discussed books. They would read the same book and discuss it. They stayed close emotionally despite great physical distances. Could there be anything more romantic for book lovers than discussing books through letters?

The former city girl was now a fully fledged homesteader living in an island wilderness while raising three young children on her own. Yet she somehow found time to decorate their kitchen, take the kids to the beach, teach her middle daughter to read, and keep the garden productive. She got used to not hearing from Roderick for weeks. And she got used to worrisome news. One letter reported he had catarrhal jaundice and had been shipped back to the Vernon military hospital. He recovered. Relief.

Ann was marvellously adaptive. She sold her car when gas rationing and expensive repairs made it impractical to keep. Her beloved Ford, that she had bought with her bookstore earnings before marriage and that they took on their honeymoon, was gone. What do you do when you don't have a car? Turn to two wheels! Ann rode her bike with her youngest son on the back and taught her older daughter to ride a bike of her own.

Ann was a key person in her community, and this didn't stop when Roderick was away. Perhaps the most impressive of her accomplishments during the war was that she stayed involved in her own hobbies and interests. She was hospital auxiliary president, attended peace advocate meetings, and helped with school sports days. She hired a babysitter so she could canvas for the Red Cross, and she was a Scout leader and a member of the Catholic Women's League, Voice of Women, Parent-Teacher Association, and Campbell River Recreational Association.

Later in her life, Ann sat on the board of Strathcona Park Lodge, an outdoor education centre, which still exists today. She was also on the John Howard Society board and volunteered at Parents in Crisis, an organization that helped parents cope with anger toward their children in safe and productive ways. Ann's ability to care for her family while maintaining her own identity and interests was truly inspiring.

After three years away, Roderick came home. He had witnessed war, undergone minor surgeries, and damaged a disk in his back, but he was home. With Roderick home, Ann could take bus and ferry trips to visit friends in the Lower Mainland.

Despite Ann's life of advocacy and service to others, Roderick Haig-Brown is better known than his wife. He was a judge, university chancellor, army officer, radio broadcaster, conservationist, fly fisherman, and author of thirty-one books. Ann had a major part in those books, as she was Roderick's typist and a driving force behind his published works. She would type and retype manuscripts, this being before copy machines existed. Like so many women of her time, she is an unsung heroine.

The couple supported each other in everything. Ann had immense reverence for Roderick's books and work. And he had the utmost respect for her. In *Measure of the Year*, Roderick writes: "She was a convinced intellectual, better read than most professors of English, altogether confidently and securely of the great world." He is quoted as saying that he married an intellectual far better read and artistically far more sophisticated than himself. He respected her opinion always and was eternally grateful that his wife was educated, intellectually stimulating, and supportive. His equal in every way.

Ann somehow balanced work and her family with a vibrant social life. Above Tide had a well-frequented guest room. It hosted Ann's mother, her or Roderick's siblings, or their friends. Ann even hosted local women who needed a safe place to sleep. It was a precursor of a safe house for women named after her. A journalist who had recently moved to Campbell River wrote about Ann in her column in the *Vancouver Sun*: "How DOES she do it!... When you drop in unexpectedly... Ann may be scrubbing floors, milking cows, perched up on the topmost pear tree, feeding chickens or shooing the sheep out of the vegetable garden, but the minute a guest appears, Ann drops everything, slips into a clean frock, smears on some lipstick and proceeds to while away the rest of the day entertaining you as if she had a flock of servants looking after all those chores you guiltily realize you are keeping her from."

In 1959 Ann started working at the high school in Campbell River. She began by covering for absent teachers, but ended up a librarian, making the library the pride and joy of the school. She was known for bestowing a love of books on her students and for her genuine care for her students. Ann retired when she was sixty-eight—but she didn't slow down. She and Roderick travelled all over Canada and the United States to promote his books and conservation work.

One Saturday morning in 1976, Ann, now sixty-eight, stepped onto the back porch of Above Tide to call Roderick for lunch. As he turned to her, he fell to the ground. He passed away instantly of a heart attack. The love of her life was gone. The man with whom she had started a new life in Canada, her equal and her co-parent, the man who gave her gifts of satin nightgowns and slippers in exactly her size, her biggest fan and supporter, was gone.

A few days later, Ann scattered Roderick's ashes over daffodils that he had planted only weeks earlier. Words of love had held them together and books had bonded them throughout their life. The books and words Roderick had written kept his memory alive in Ann's sharp mind and beautiful heart after he died.

Ann was resiliently determined to enjoy life despite her sudden loss. She travelled. She learned to paint. She went to Italy and learned to speak Italian. She travelled to see azalea and rhododendron gardens in the southeast United States. She visited her children and grandchildren, the eldest of whom was also named Ann, and attended their weddings and commencements. She journeyed to England to visit Roderick's sisters.

Ann was active into old age. Despite health issues like poly-myalgia, pneumonia, arthritis, and a hysterectomy because of can-cer, she was determined to be involved in her community. She counted in Italian for her physio exercises. She kept gardening and doing minor repairs around her house. She hosted family, refin-ished furniture, and spent ample time with her grandchildren. In 1993 she was flown by helicopter to Haida Gwaii to join David Suzuki in celebrating its new national park status.

In her later years, Ann helped with the library at a women's safe house that was named after her. The women and their children called her Granny Ann. She was known for being a gifted listener. Later in life she became involved in the Cystic Fibrosis Society of BC, Friends of Schizophrenics, and Kingfisher Creek Ecological Reserve—a protected area near her property. She celebrated her eightieth birthday in her garden surrounded by grandchildren.

Above Tide still stands next to the river in Campbell River, BC—midway up Vancouver Island. In summer it houses bed and breakfast guests. In winter it welcomes writers-in-residence, who write words and craft masterpieces at Roderick's former desk.

Ann's name has been applied to a mountain, a transition house for women, a day of celebration in Campbell River, a cabin at a wilderness lodge, and her beloved homestead. If someone wanted to explore Ann's area, they could hike Mount Haig-Brown, stay in the Haig-Brown cabin at Strathcona Park Lodge, or stay overnight at the Haig-Brown House Bed and Breakfast. The Haig-Brown name remains strong. The Ann Elmore Transition House opened in 1987 to provide a safe place for women and children fleeing abusive situations. Open still, it offers a variety of support options for individuals.

In 2008 the Mayor of Campbell River declared May 3 as Ann Elmore Day. This day features exhibits at the museum and a tea at Above Tide to celebrate Ann and her immense contributions to Campbell River. A Fall Festival is held each fall at the Haig-Brown House. It celebrates environmental stewardship, community, fly fishing, and local artisans, and features music, an artisan market, food, and guided tours of the house. Wooden book shelves still house a collection of the four thousand books Ann and Roderick collected together.

ANN PASSED AWAY in 1990 at Vancouver General Hospital due to a blood clot in her leg. She was eighty-two years old. Her ashes were scattered beside Roderick's. I imagine them reunited in another place—reading, discussing books, gardening—no longer apart and keeping in touch by love letter.

14

Elizabeth Quocksister
Cultural Teacher and Photographer

ELIZABETH QUOCKSISTER WAS many things: cultural teacher, community leader, dancer, nurse, mother of ten, and photographer. Her photographs preserved moments, displayed changing ways of life, and promoted culture. She loved music, dance, and traditional food. She witnessed enormous changes in her life but throughout it all wanted people to get along in harmony. She advocated for people of any cultural background to be able to learn about Indigenous cultures.

ELIZABETH GORDON GLENDALE was born in Knight Inlet, 80 kilometres north of Campbell River on BC's central coast, in 1925. Her mother was Katherine Henderson, a midwife from Alert Bay who lived to be 104; her father was George Glendale, a hereditary Chief. Elizabeth's home Nation was the Da'naxda'xw Nation, whose traditional territory lies in Knight Inlet.

Being the eldest child of high-ranking parents, Elizabeth was considered a princess and had ten princess names. With this inherited honour came a large copper shield that represented tradition, power, prestige, and wealth. She was thus said to be "born into the copper." Hereditary status always goes to the eldest sibling, with other siblings not having the same honours.

When Elizabeth was ten years old, missionaries from a residential school came for the children of her village. Elizabeth and her family knew only too well that the missionaries would take the children from their parents and forbid them from honouring their language and culture. Young Elizabeth hid under her mother's long dress when the missionaries came to the door. Not noticing her, the missionaries left. However, on a subsequent visit they succeeded in capturing Elizabeth and taking her to St. Michael's Residential School in Alert Bay. The residential schools were places of abuse, suffering, and horrific treatment—shameful marks on Canada's history.

Years later, Elizabeth met a man named George Quocksister at a community event in Campbell River. George had attended the same residential school as Elizabeth and was a hereditary Chief from Campbell River. During his time at residential school, he and his younger brother were constantly hungry; they ate moldy bread and regularly found bugs in their oatmeal bowls. They remembered their father telling them not to eat anything bad, so (like many) they decided to run away. They took shoes, bread, and water and left secretly in a dugout canoe. After paddling over seventy kilometres north, they landed in Kelsey Bay, near Sayward. The boys hid the dugout and then began hitchhiking, only to be picked up

Elizabeth Quocksister

Elizabeth Quocksister. IMAGE 020391-410
COURTESY OF THE MUSEUM AT CAMPBELL RIVER

by police, who laughed and took them to a Port Alberni residential school. George eventually left residential school when he turned fifteen by convincing the judge that if they let him go, he would become a commercial fisherman and wouldn't be a burden on society. He fished for seventy-two years and made a very good living.

Elizabeth and George married in 1946 and had ten children together. They vowed none of their children would attend residential school—and none of them did. Some went to college and others became top-notch skippers on fishing boats.

Both Elizabeth and George were extremely hard-working. George fished his entire life, and Elizabeth had a variety of jobs. She worked with George on fish boats. She worked at canneries in Bella Bella and Ocean Falls. She worked as a nurse's aide at Lourdes Hospital in Campbell River. All while running a household, caring for the homeless and less fortunate members of her community, and promoting traditional culture and language.

She also found time for a hobby: photography. She had received a camera as a gift and used it to take striking photos wherever she went. A collection of her photos from between 1940 and 1960 are part of an online collection belonging to the Museum at Campbell River. They do exactly what excellent photos should do: capture the moment, make you feel something, and tell a story. They teach something about that time, beginning from when Campbell River's population was under two thousand and the Island Highway was a single lane road. To say they show great change is an understatement. Some of the photos are family portraits, taken in the doorway of a house, on a bench in Kingcome Inlet doing what families do—smiling, laughing, arms draped casually over one another.

Elizabeth's photos show mundane life moments in a fresh way. Cute children crowded together on a porch. People at work—fishing, or working in the Bones Bay Cannery in Johnstone Strait. Miss Campbell River beauty pageant contestants in a fancy convertible. A Canada Day parade. They also tell stories of injustice and sadness. They represent times of rampant racism. Photos taken before 1950 feature Indigenous children who couldn't attend public schools and adults who couldn't practise their culture, vote, or be considered citizens of Canada.

Elizabeth Quocksister

Her photograph collection shows remarkable contrast and variety. A woman in front of an intricately carved totem pole; a man in a sleek and shiny car. A child, bicycle at his side and cedar bark gathering basket on his back; two teenagers sitting in the grass, very evidently in love. A woman standing on her porch, leaning on a pole and looking dreamily at the camera while a little girl in gumboots and braids tugs at the hem of her dress, vying for her attention.

All this without any formal training.

Elizabeth was also deeply involved in preserving her local language and culture and spoke both Kwaḵwala and English fluently. She learned ancient songs and dances and taught them to others, including her children, after anti-potlatch legislation was repealed. A talented seamstress, she also taught her children how to sew traditional regalia.

When Elizabeth's children were young, adults in the community were careful not to speak Kwaḵwala in front of their children. This was because if children were found speaking Kwaḵwala, the parents would be arrested. Elizabeth valued her language so much that she went with other community members to speak their language in an orchard near their homes. The orchard was chosen because it was out of earshot of the children.

Traditional food was a big part of Elizabeth's life. She survived off the land. Her children remember Elizabeth in her garden, growing beets, potatoes, corn, and string beans. Her son George described the land as being a "candy store," covered with berry bushes, apple trees, and pear trees. Elizabeth smoked fish and canned various foods—salmon, deer, fruits, and vegetables—and loved making desserts. She often made soft baked apples filled with sweet brown sugar. At Halloween, she made candy apples—a tradition still going strong in her community today.

ELIZABETH'S LEGACY INCLUDES helping others whenever she could. A major way in which she changed the lives of others was by saving many girls from the horrors of residential school. She would find babysitting work for girls from St. Michael's Residential School, which helped them escape. They could then return to their family, community, and culture, free to move on with their lives.

In 2008 Elizabeth was recognized by the City of Campbell River. They honoured her with a Community Builder Award for her public service and selfless contribution to the betterment of the City of Campbell River. She was the founding member of a group of people keeping culture and language alive. Her children said she started the traditions of Easter egg hunts and Christmas trees in downtown Campbell River. Every Christmas Elizabeth would bring a box of cookies to each household, with her daughter Carol and son George assisting her.

In July 1981, Elizabeth's children describe her as "going home to the Creator." She was fifty-four years old and had had cancer. Her husband, George, followed her in 2017.

Elizabeth's legacy lives on through her children. George Quocksister Jr., Carol Bear, and Louella Serhan are all involved in their community. Louella designed regalia with her late mom and knows all the designs. Carol was recognized by the City of Campbell River in 2016 for her leadership in initiatives like Walk Away from Racism and other events by Kwakiutl District Council. Like their mother, Carol and Louella do all they can to maintain their culture by sharing what they know, by teaching singing and dancing, and sewing button blankets. George Jr. is a hereditary Chief and committed environmental activist. He works with the marine conservation NGO Sea Shepherd to fight against fish farms, which he sees as taking away livelihoods and food sources—not only fish stocks but also clams and prawns.

The children remember their late mom as a hard worker who was friends with all. They remember her being brilliantly smart, with her education coming from reading books. They remember her being left-handed, valuing education, taking them by bus to pick strawberries in summers, and being gifted at teaching culture. She loved music and played the mouth harp, harmonica, and accordion. Elizabeth and George survived off the land and worked together always. Their children remember them holding hands together as best friends. Both did very well for themselves financially. Elizabeth had absolute respect for her culture and believed everyone should be able to learn about other cultures.

Elizabeth Quocksister was a remarkable woman whose legacy of cultural teaching and photos are truly admirable. They chronicled changing times and add to the understanding of history. And it can be argued that a better understanding of history can contribute to reconciliation—which is vital to a healthy, equitable society.

15

Lilian Bland
Aviatrix and Journalist

LILIAN BLAND SPENT hours watching black gulls surf wind currents, high above the cliffs of the Scottish island where she lived. She daydreamed of flying like them. In 1910 her dreams became reality when she became the first woman in the world to design, build, and fly her own plane.

When most people think of female pilots, Amelia Earhart's name usually comes to mind. However, there was an even more daring, albeit lesser known, innovative aviatrix: Lilian Bland. Even lesser known is this European woman's connection to a remote coastal inlet on northern Vancouver Island.

"Aviatrix" is an outdated word for a female pilot, but that was how Lilian was known in her day. Her first flight was just seven years after the Wright brothers flew a plane for the first time. Most women weren't even driving cars; Lilian was flying a plane.

Lilian Bland

LILIAN BLAND WAS born in Kent, England, in 1878. Her mother died when Lilian was young, and her artist father took her with him on his travels around the world. Lilian described her upbringing in a letter to a former work contact named Mr. Mees:

I for my part was also studying life. My mother was a society woman, my father was an artist, and with these two opposite interests I saw both sides of life, the Bohemian and the Fashionable. From the start I had a thirst for knowledge and a strong dislike for "society," their empty lives, empty talk, fashions, gambling etc. Before I was twenty I had been to many of the cities of Europe, studied art in Paris, studied music in Rome, life everywhere, studied the various religious sects, ancient and modern, read the works of the philosophers of Germany, France and Italy and found no truth or satisfaction in them, and finally came back to Ireland where my father had settled down with his sister.

It's safe to say Lilian's childhood was unconventional.

Lilian worked as a journalist from 1903 to 1908, writing instructional articles about car racing, hunting, hunting by horseback, horse jumping, and how to fall off a horse with minimal injury. Having injured herself riding, she insisted on riding horses astride. A priest in Tipperary once told people to stone her for riding astride in a man's saddle. To Lilian's delight, the people cheered her on instead.

Her flying fixation came about from watching black gulls and seeing a postcard of Louis Blériot's 1909 flight over the English Channel. She desperately wanted to fly but couldn't find anyone to teach her. Finally, she took matters into her own hands. She built a glider and hired the garden boy to be her mechanic. She bought a twenty-horsepower engine and didn't give up, even after the props flew off in splinters during testing. She named her plane *The Mayfly*. Its first flight was in a bull pasture, complete with an aggravated bull to add to the adventure.

Lilian's father desperately wanted her to stop flying and tried to bribe her into doing so by buying her a Ford Model T. The *Mayfly* frame was given to a gliding club, the engine was sold, and Lilian moved onto other adventures, including working as the first female agent for Ford in Ireland. When asked about flying, she said she had done it as an experiment.

What brought this eccentric aviatrix and journalist to northern Vancouver Island? A search for freedom and her vagabond husband Charles Loftus Bland. Charles Bland had been the outcast of his family. After a time in the army, stints in an asylum, and potato-picking jobs, his family sent Charles to Canada, not so unusual a move in those days. Charles farmed an orange grove and gold mined in California, finally moving with some buddies to homestead at Quatsino Sound. Quatsino Sound is a set of coastal inlets on northwest Vancouver Island. To reach Quatsino, one drives north from Victoria, to nearly the north end of Vancouver Island. Head west from there, and you travel by boat from Port Alice or Coal Harbour to the hamlet of Quatsino.

Charles was twenty-six years old when he arrived in Quatsino Sound in 1907. On his new property, he cleared stumps and built a hand-hewn log cabin, living off the land and his small army pension. In 1911 he returned to England briefly and somewhat spontaneously married Lilian. By this time, Lilian was thirty-two

Lilian Bland and Mayfly. WWW.LILIANBLAND.IE

and Charles was twenty-nine. A year after getting married, Lilian emigrated to BC and joined Charles at Quatsino. They kept their marriage secret for an unusual reason: their fathers were brothers, making them first cousins.

Homesteading life at Quatsino was arduous. Clearing stumps for gardens was back-breaking work and there was endless wood to chop. No roads connected to the outside world; getting anywhere involved boating. Their marriage was turbulent. Wolves howled outside their cabin. Money was tight. To boost their income they turned to brewing and selling loganberry wine to the Central Hotel on Limestone Island (now called Drake Island), just south of Quatsino. This was the era of prohibition. Police from Port Alice caught Charles, and he paid a $300 fine rather than spending thirty days in jail.

In 1913 Lilian had a baby girl they named Patricia. Lilian took many photos at Quatsino, documenting many homesteading challenges that most women from where Lilian was from could barely have dreamed of. Lilian's fifteen-year-old cousin Mary Madden joined them in 1917 to help out. She brought along her young daughter.

In 1925 the family unit took a road trip in a Ford Model T. Of course, Lilian drove. It was a grand adventure that Lilian recalled fondly in a letter: "I had the trusty Ford in which the seats would turn into two beds, and a tent hooked on the side. A large kettle was slung behind, a roll of blankets on the mud-guard, the blue Jay in his cage, two children and the three of us, and left California for a 1,000-mile trip to Vancouver."

When Patricia was older, she and Lilian planned to start a fur farm together for extra income. They secured a licence and registered a trapline but would never use either.

When Patricia was sixteen years old, a wood splinter in her foot caused a tetanus infection that ultimately killed her. Lilian was understandably shattered. Grief became another burden in a life that was already exceedingly difficult. In a letter to friends in England, Lilian described Patricia: "She would have been seventeen this month, a child of the woods, a born naturalist and artist, she was yet my right hand in all practical work, with the skill and energy of an old-timer, utterly unselfish, calm and brave in the face of danger. Death in connection with one so full of life seemed impossible—unreal." Eventually, unable to bear living in a place full of memories of her deceased daughter, Lilian returned to England alone.

Lilian's cousin Mary remained in Quatsino. She and Charles married—there is no reliable record of whether this was considered a scandalous move—and had five children. Lilian had no intention of returning and Mary had committed to the home-steading lifestyle. Charles and Mary's twins were born on a boat en route to Port Alice hospital. An article in the *Daily Colonist* discusses Charles's continued grief over Patricia's death. He would apparently insert iodine into his children's cuts using a large needle, likely terrified another child would get tetanus.

Lilian found some happiness back in England, where she wore trousers, painted, gambled, gardened, and played the stock market. She didn't like talking about her time in Canada. The grief was a continual challenge, but finances were no problem. She fared well in her stock market ventures and retired in the headlands of Land's End, Cornwall, on a cliffside estate overlooking the sea. She was a spry older woman and lived alone by choice. A photo shows her bundled up in wool sweater and slacks, marching through her clifftop garden, waves riding the expansive beaches far below. In a newspaper article, she talked about gardening: "When I came back from Canada, I became a gardener... I hate people. In gardening, outdoors, you get away from them."

LILIAN BLAND PASSED away on May 11, 1971, at the age of ninety-one. She was talented in many diverse areas: equestrian, journalism, painting, gardening, photography, shooting, driving, and flying. She always felt like a black sheep and a disgrace to her family. She searched for truth and freedom, and found them—along with heartbreak—in the wilds of northern Vancouver Island.

She is remembered as the first woman to design, build, and fly a plane. Aviators still place wreaths at her grave. In 2010 multiple historical societies and aviator groups commemorated her flight one hundred years before. Lilian Bland Community Park in Glengormley, Northern Ireland, was named in her honour and features an aluminum rendition of The *Mayfly* that people can sit on and pretend to fly. The Port Hardy, BC, museum featured a Lilian Bland exhibit in 2018. Lilian Bland is remembered in both Northern Ireland and northern Vancouver Island as a pioneer homesteader and pioneer pilot. Her memory is preserved on two continents.

16

Ga'axsta'las
(Jane Constance Cook)
Land Claims Activist
and Translator/Interpreter

JANE CONSTANCE COOK (Ga'axsta'las) was a midwife, land claims advocate, women's rights advocate, mediator, translator/interpreter, mother of sixteen children, and political activist. She used her education and language abilities to fiercely advocate for her family, her community, and especially the most marginalized members of her community. Some criticized her for her views and actions, but she lived a full life of advocating for women's rights and health care access for Indigenous Peoples, fishing rights, and land claims—and left a strong and enduring legacy.

The most comprehensive overview of Ga'axsta'las's life and opinions can be found in *Standing with Ga'axsta'las: Jane Constance Cook and the Politics of Memory, Church and Custom,* written by Leslie A. Robertson in collaboration with the Chief and members of the Gix̱sa̱m Clan. The story that appears below was reviewed by Wedlidi Speck, on behalf of the Gix̱sa̱m Clan.

In Kwakwa̱ka̱'wakw culture, Ga'axsta'las's birth order as the first-born of a first-born gave her a high-ranking status within her community. Her most controversial act was speaking out against early-twentieth-century potlatches; her power lay in speaking both Kwak̓wala and English fluently.

IN ABOUT 1870 Jane Constance Gilbert was born in Port Blakely, on Bainbridge Island, in Washington's Puget Sound. Her mother was Emily Wanukw, a high-ranking first-born Kwakwa̱ka̱'wakw woman. Her father was an English sailor named William Gilbert who piloted ships from Port Townsend up to Alaska. The two met in Victoria, BC. In addition to her English name, Jane had a Kwakwa̱ka̱'wakw one: Ga'axsta'las.

Some think Ga'axsta'las spent some of her childhood at sea on her father's schooner. If so, it would have had to have been before 1912, the year William Gilbert died. She likely spent time in Port Townsend, Washington, then Victoria, and then Fort Rupert (near present-day Port Hardy). She was certainly in Fort Rupert in 1881, as she is listed on its 1881 census.

In 1879, when Ga'axsta'las was about nine, the Canadian government passed the *Indian Act*. This gave the government total control over most aspects of Indigenous Peoples' lives, including control over land, education, resources, wills, self-government, and who could legally lay claim to Indigenous status. Indigenous children were taken from their families and communities and placed in residential schools to forcibly assimilate them into the

Ga'axsta'las (Jane Constance Cook)

Ga' axsta'las, Jane Constance Cook in Alert Bay.
IMAGE H-07220 COURTESY OF THE BC MUSEUM AND ARCHIVES

newcomers' culture. Centuries-old cultural practices were prohibited. Indigenous people who went to university lost their status. Women who married non-Indigenous men lost their status, as did their children. Indigenous men who married non-Indigenous women were free to keep their Indigenous status and even pass it on to their wives.

Ga'axsta'las arrived in Alert Bay in 1879. There, she lived in Alfred Hall's mission house and attended the Indian Girls' Mission residential school. Ga'axsta'las and Stephen Cook, who was known primarily by his English name, met around 1881. They had been childhood peers in Alert Bay, as he had attended the Indian Boys' Mission residential school. Both these schools were run by a couple named Alfred and Elizabeth Hall. Stephen and Ga'axsta'las spoke Kwak̓wala fluently, but speaking the Kwak̓wala language was later banned at a new residential school called St. Michael's Anglican residential school that opened later in 1929. In addition to their shared language, Stephen and Ga'axsta'las also both occupied high positions in their respective families.

In 1888 Ga'axsta'las and Stephen were married in Alert Bay. Afterward, Ga'axsta'las made the unusual, and controversial, decision to leave the potlatch system, which was primarily, but not exclusively, aimed at the redistribution of wealth among a community. Although she and Stephen had been "children of the potlatch system," they decided not to follow the custom in their own marriage. She disagreed with the custom of getting married multiple times for the sake of bringing wealth and prestige to a woman's family. Ga'axsta'las's Christian faith, acquired during her time at residential school, likely influenced this decision, along with a desire to remain married to Stephen.

Renouncing the potlatch custom was a serious act of rebellion for a high-ranking, first-born woman. It was also the first of many decisions Ga'axsta'las made to stay true to her beliefs. She was criticized her whole adult life because of her decision to marry only once, as many first-born noble women married multiple times to accumulate wealth for their fathers. The couple had sixteen children together, and one of their daughters would later guide Emily Carr (page 22) on a painting trip.

Ga'axsta'las's ability to speak both English and Kwak̓wala put her in a unique position. At a time of many court hearings and much political shifting, she could interpret both languages, putting her in a relatively powerful position. From 1910 onwards, she not only interpreted at court trials and hearings, but also translated and interpreted speeches and church sermons. Her involvement in the community was far-reaching. She was the president of the Anglican Women's Auxiliary for thirty years. This group started in 1895 and offered support to women and young mothers in Alert Bay. Ga'axsta'las was the only woman on the elected committee of Allied Indian Tribes of British Columbia, a political organization of Chiefs and Indigenous leaders. She was also involved in the Native Brotherhood, fighting for Indigenous people's right to have Canadian citizenship while retaining their Indigenous status and maintaining hereditary privileges.

Her advocacy covered a variety of political issues including land, health care, fishing and resource rights, language and cultural rights, and the well-being of women and children. She spoke out against tuberculosis hospitals and campaigned for nonracist health services, translated powerful Chiefs' words on land claims, and fought for support for destitute women and children. She apparently became a self-taught nurse from reading medical books. It's said she delivered her first baby at seventeen years old, after a woman went into labour on an Alert Bay beach, and we know that she was still delivering babies into her seventies. She accompanied missionary doctors to remote villages as an interpreter. She sat with sick and dying community members. She provided emotional support whenever and wherever it was needed. She helped people grieve. She even provided marriage counselling.

Her advocacy around potlatching was the most controversial part of Ga'axsta'las's life and was something that at times created problems for her and her family. Potlatches were central to Kwakwaka'wakw culture. They centred around gift giving by high-ranking members of a community to express goodwill toward the other members of that community; in doing so, the gift givers confirmed their social status and ultimately contributed to strengthening relationships in and between communities. Nowadays, potlatches mean different things to different people.

Potlatches were banned by the Canadian government in 1884, but instead of dying out, they went underground. At the time of the ban, people became divided into potlatchers and anti-potlatchers. Ga'axsta'las was an unapologetic anti-potlatcher. She saw them as unfavourable to women and children, and disagreed with the practice of women and children from first marriages being cast aside and made destitute when a man remarried. She believed potlatches gave men elevated status while women and children were left with limited options. She didn't agree with men marrying strategically to increase their and their family's wealth while women and children's well-being was not considered. She didn't agree with underage brides—girls—being married without their consent. She wanted women to have a right to choose their marriage partner and to have a say in their own marriages. She worried about the increasing number of women working in the sex trade in the United States. She disagreed with sham marriages, which were annulled after the transfer of privilege and properties.

Ga'axsta'las was deeply proud of her education and used it for good. Her literacy skills meant she could write letters—to the Superintendent of Indian Affairs, Indian agents, sawmill managers, and police officers—for community members, to voice her opinions, and point out injustices. She wrote to Anglican bishops on behalf of Kwakwaka'wakw communities to recognize their rights, including the right to compensation for land they had lost. She wrote letters on behalf of female relatives, voicing concerns about the exploitive nature and legality of their marriages. She wrote letters asking why women were being fined for buying liquor, an infraction at the time, but the men selling them the liquor were not, and to point out when a woman was being married to a man who had two wives already.

Around 1913 Ga'axsta'las was sworn in as an interpreter and tribal representative for the McKenna-McBride Royal Commission. This commission involved both the federal and provincial governments and was set up to address the question of the allocation of reserve lands for Indigenous Peoples. Ga'axsta'las spoke out against proposed reductions in reserve lands. She fought for better access to medical services and education for her people; for timber, food, and hunting and fishing rights; for land where her people could harvest clams, harvest timber, pick berries, hunt, fish eulachon, and live. She fought for the rights of local Indigenous Peoples to fish for food and participate in commercial fisheries (a right accorded to Japanese- and European-descent people). She fought for housing rights on reserves, so the people living there could build and own a house. When she noticed Indigenous people getting poor service in hospitals due to racism, she advocated for equitable health care.

GA'AXSTA'LAS EXPERIENCED MANY personal hardships. Three of her sons died—one from tuberculosis and one dysentery, and one died on active service in the First World War. In the 1920s, two of her daughters passed away. At times her views on the potlatch meant she and her family were isolated from their community. A strong Christian faith kept her going through her hardships. A firm sense of justice kept her focused. And adaptability kept her rolling with the massive changes she saw in her lifetime—whether it was the introduction of electricity or wide-reaching political changes.

She lived through what some Kwakwaka'wakw people call the dark years. Years of missionaries, smallpox epidemics, grief, loss, residential schools, colonialism, and government restrictions on access to the natural resources Indigenous people had been using sustainably for thousands of years. Throughout these times, she cared deeply for her family and community. People remember her as having incredibly accurate foresight and a deep-rooted pride in her education and for encouraging her grandchildren to look to their futures.

Ga'axsta'las was a feminist in the most literal way: she acted for and about women. She dedicated her life to fighting for women to have social, political, and economic equity with men, and to have the right to choose who they married. Living in a Eurocentric, male-dominated society, Ga'axsta'las frequently stood up to very powerful white men—politicians, police chiefs, Indian Affair officials, missionaries, and bishops. She challenged patriarchal authority figures and would not be intimidated, and is remembered for her physical and mental strength. Well spoken and articulate, she was said to have commanded attention when speaking, no matter who the audience was. She spoke for the most vulnerable people of her community when they most needed a voice.

In 1951, Ga'axsta'las died of a heart attack at the age of eighty-two. She and Stephen had been married for sixty-three years. She had fifty grandchildren and twenty-six great-grandchildren, who lovingly referred to her as Granny Cook. Many of Ga'axsta'las's relatives still hold positions of power in Alert Bay, either as hereditary

Ga'axsta'las (Jane Constance Cook)

Chiefs or active members in their community. Her great-grandson Wedlidi Speck has done much to promote reconciliation and cultural safety. Ga'axsta'las is still remembered as a strong Indigenous activist. She read extensively and thought deeply. She worked hard and advocated tirelessly for her community. In Ga'axsta'las's obituary, her niece Ellen Neel described her as "Calm, serene, dignified, [and] a tower of strength to all who knew her."

CHAPTER

17

Ellen Gibbs
Cape Scott Pioneer

THERE WAS REGULAR homesteading and then there was next-level homesteading on northern Vancouver Island. Ellen Gibbs undertook both. She was among the second wave of brave pioneers who attempted to settle and build a thriving community at Cape Scott—at the very northern tip of Vancouver Island. A wet and harsh potential Utopia, where settlers battled against intense isolation, stormy seas, thick rainforest, bold cougars, and failed government promises.

ELLEN GIBBS WAS born Ellen Tippett in 1886. Her parents were John and Mary Ann Tippett of Cornwall, England. The couple was married in Cornwall and had their first three children there. The rest of their seven children, including Ellen, were born in Canada. The family moved first to Pennsylvania in 1873, where Ellen's father worked in the copper mines, and later to Nanaimo, where he helped build Haliburton Street in south Nanaimo and worked as a coal miner.

The final move for the Tippett family was to Nanoose Bay in 1883, where Ellen's father bought farm property under the *Free Land Homestead Act* of 1872. Under this act, settlers were able to purchase acres of land at a good price with one stipulation: they must occupy and improve it. When the family first moved to Nanoose from Nanaimo, they arrived by boat. After that, travelling between Nanoose and Nanaimo involved a lengthy horse and buggy journey through thick forest.

Nanoose, which lies between Nanaimo and Parksville on Nanoose Bay, is the traditional territory of the Snaw-Naw-As Nation, who have lived there for thousands of years. It is an area of plentiful natural resources—thick forests, abundant clams and oysters, fish in crystal-clear creeks, flocks of geese, plentiful wild game like deer and elk, and salal berries, which were boiled, dried, and transformed into square cakes. When the first European settlers arrived, they formed a close-knit community who would share a deer they hunted, as nobody had a way to preserve or refrigerate it. In winter, cougars, bears, and wolves strutted fearlessly into the community from the surrounding mountains.

The Tippetts were one of the early settler families in Nanoose, and one of Ellen's sisters, Jenny, was one of the first non-Indigenous babies born there. Her brother Charles was also born on the Nanoose family farm.

As a child, Ellen was a great help on the farm. Her rough-and-tumble upbringing made her robust and she was well built. Her skirt was in constant need of mending from being ripped while bringing in cattle. She was known to hide out-of-season birds in her skirt

Driftwood fence and hay field at sand neck between
Guise Bay and Experiment. IMAGE B-01529
COURTESY OF THE BC MUSEUM AND ARCHIVES

when she saw the local constable coming. Her hardy disposition would serve her well in her future life. But she was also charismatic and tender. The Snaw-Naw-As people of the area apparently loved her. One family even named their daughter Ellen after her.

Wilfred (Billy) Gibbs was another Nanoose Bay homesteader. He was an ex-British Royal Navy sailor who had sailed from England. He arrived by ship to Victoria and made his way to Nanaimo to work in the coal mines. He arrived in Nanoose in 1901 with his friend Percy LeMare. Together they bought fifty-two acres of land and built a small cabin on it. Billy lived there until he got married to a fellow Nanoose Bay homesteader—Ellen Tippett.

Ellen and Billy were married in 1905, when Ellen was eighteen. They were a hard-working pair. A photo shows them haying as a team—Ellen powerfully perched atop the hay wagon wielding a pitch fork and Billy standing beside it. Billy occasionally worked as a miner at the Wellington coal mines of Nanaimo.

In 1908 adventure came calling to Ellen and Billy. Billy's friend Theodore Frederiksen and some Danish settlers were making a homesteading attempt on the very northern tip of Vancouver Island in a community called Cape Scott. Ellen and Billy headed north.

The first settlers in Cape Scott had been Danish fishermen Nels Jensen and Rasmus Hansen in 1898. They hatched a dream of a Utopian community after discovering fertile meadowland, a sheltered lagoon, and pristine forests while travelling around the area by ship. By 1899 Cape Scott had a store, sawmill, boat mooring area, telegraph office, community hall, newspaper, post office, and school. The pioneers were excellent farmers and their farms were productive. However, without a road they had nowhere to sell their produce. Undaunted, they held onto the government promise of a road and continued attracting more settlers to grow their community.

Ellen and Billy were among the second group of settlers trying to make a go of it at Cape Scott. They moved there with their four daughters—Ellen was born in 1907, Dorothy in 1908, Ada in 1910, and Alice in 1913—around the time that Cape Scott's population was at its peak. The pioneers were determined to persevere through wet weather, storms, broken dykes, and the constant concern over cougars who killed domestic livestock and ate wild game they hunted.

Billy fished, worked as a road boss, and worked on the telephone line to Shushartie Bay. Ellen had many roles at Cape Scott. Along with raising her four daughters, she was the community veterinarian, builder, hunter, midwife, and even dentist. She had an old-fashioned pair of dental pliers she used to extract teeth. Who knows where she acquired these pliers, but they must have resembled some metal tool from a garage sale pile. Those were the days of "street dentistry," when local blacksmiths or barbers conducted unlicensed dentistry. Cape Scott had no blacksmith or barber, but they did have Ellen Gibbs. The cure back then for toothache or decay was to remove the troubling tooth. This would have been done without sedation, painkillers, or proper sterilization of the dental pliers between uses.

Ellen must have had strong hands and a strong stomach to extract teeth with her pliers. It would have taken an enormous amount of force to pull out a tooth—even a rotten one—and it would have been horrific to cause someone such excruciating pain. Ellen extracted many teeth from community members mouths. People apparently came from as far as Holberg, San Josef, and Alert Bay to have their rotten teeth extracted by her. Alert Bay to Cape Scott is nearly a hundred kilometres and would have involved a boat trip, seeing as Alert Bay is an island community.

Ellen also loved hunting and was a sharpshooter. She provided deer, ducks, and other wild game for her family and others. Her daughter Dorothy told a reporter for the *Daily Colonist* about her mother's hunting prowess: "She was a very good hunter... she used to go down to the flats at the head of the lagoon and catch hold of a cow's collar. The she would hide behind it, using it as a blind while she prodded it close to where there were ducks or geese. We were never short of meat when she was able to get out hunting." In the same article, Dorothy recalls when the dozen cows the Gibbs family owned were heard fighting out in the barn. Ellen stated she would put an end to the noise, grabbed her hand saw, and marched out toward the barn. She returned, covered in blood from head to toe. The cows no longer had horns with which to fight.

Cape Scott life was hard. Mail arrived by trail or sea only. Log cabins were built with hand-split cedar. Children filled the chinks with moss and ate syrup sandwiches and cranberry jam sandwiches, with the jam made from the cranberries that grew in the peat bogs. Families farmed vegetables and livestock. Staple essentials were delivered once a month by steamer—weather permitting. One Christmas, the ship coming from Shushartie to Fisherman's Cove with Christmas toys and supplies was wrecked, much to the disappointment of the Cape Scott children.

There were good times too. The annual fall fairs. All-night dances with fiddle and accordion music in the community hall that also served as the school house. The tide that gifted pioneers with fresh oranges of mysterious origin. Children of Cape Scott playing on white-sand beaches and sand necks, finding shiny, emerald coloured glass balls that had been used to float Japanese fishing nets and had floated all the way from Japan—the ultimate beachcomber's treasure and a cherished find to this day.

The fate of the community hinged increasingly on one thing: a road. A road would allow them to sell their produce and farm goods and give them access to the outside world. The road had been promised, and a wagon road from Holberg gave the settlers some hope, but it never materialized. There is still no road to Cape Scott. People wishing to visit this special place must get there on their own two feet.

One day it all became too much for the Gibbs. Lack of opportunities for their daughters prompted the move, but it's likely the Gibbs, like many, were done with the hardships of Cape Scott. Ellen vowed that when her youngest daughter was big enough to walk the distance, they would leave. Eventually they did just that.

Packing as much as they could on their backs and into their arms, the Gibbs family left Cape Scott on foot. One box they carried held three white cats. Many of their possessions were left behind.

The path they took along the coastline is now a coastal hiking trail called the North Coast Trail. Partway into their journey, Ellen fell on a slippery log while crossing a stream, badly spraining her ankle. For ten days, while her ankle healed enough to walk, the family camped under the stars at Cache Creek (now known as the Stranby River). They would likely have slept on the ground with no tents or lightweight air mattresses, and certainly no down sleeping bags. The family eventually arrived at their destination of Shushartie Bay, about fifty kilometres east of Cape Scott. A coastal steamer carried them away from the site of their epic experience.

ELLEN, BILLY, AND their daughters moved briefly to Vanderhoof in northern BC and then back to Nanoose. By this time it was the 1930s and they had sold their property and bought some of Ellen's father's land. They built a cottage, but eventually moved to the current day Tippett House on a hillside on the east side of modern day Northwest Bay Road. Tippett House, which is still standing, was a post office for several years, as Billy had taken on the role of postmaster. He was also a Justice of the Peace.

Ellen and Billy lived in Nanoose until their respective deaths in in 1937 and 1947. Ellen and Billy's daughter Alice Gibbs McMillan inherited the house and part of the property. Life in the country wasn't for her, so she sold it to Theordore Frederiksen, the catalyst for their Cape Scott adventure.

The cedar fences along the sand dunes that line the turquoise-green waters of Guise Bay are much photographed. Once, these fences stood strong and held livestock; now they lean, burdened with Styrofoam buoys washed up from sea, getting pummelled by winter storms and ocean winds.

Ellen Gibbs was the pioneering spirit incarnate. She confronted uncertainty and adventure head on when she joined the Cape Scott settlement. Some remember her as the strongest woman they had ever met and one who was able to fix anything—from cedar fences to complications during childbirth. She endured hardships, both physical and mental, but she stepped up and did what had to be done, no matter the situation. Ellen was a strong woman in both body and spirit. She was an indestructible strand of the Cape Scott tapestry—an adventure tale of stubborn optimism in the face of many major challenges.

Conclusion

SO, THERE YOU have it. Seventeen true stories of Vancouver Island women who boldly lived life on their own terms. You've reached the end of a journey. A voyage that started on southern Vancouver Island in Victoria and progressed up Vancouver Island until you reached Cape Scott, at the very northern tip of Vancouver Island. You've gotten to know seventeen determined women who gave themselves permission to let go of who they—and their families and society—thought they were supposed to be and become who they truly were.

Vancouver Island has always been a special place. A land of richness, in terms of physical beauty, culture, and spirit. A place of do-it-yourself, make-your-own-luck, self-sufficiency, and adventure. The women in this book embody many of those characteristics. The common threads holding them together are their determination, originality, and shining authenticity.

There are certainly other women out there whose stories are at risk of being forgotten. Perhaps I didn't stumble upon them because their stories exist only as snippets of information in archives or are briefly mentioned in an obscure and outdated book. Or perhaps they're part of a story that has been passed down in oral storytelling. I am certain I missed some noteworthy wild women whose life events, for whatever reason, weren't documented in places I could find them.

Feminist and social activist Gloria Steinem said that women have always been an equal part of the past, but they haven't been an equal part of history. I wonder if women's history will be equally and better documented in fifty or one hundred years from now. Will the Internet change how women's stories are told and maintained? Or will the unique and amazing stories of these women be lost in the sheer volume of information found on the Internet? Only time will tell.

Living life on your own terms means different things to different people. Maybe it means seeking adventure and creating experiences that align with your values—whatever those may be. Maybe it means exploring and defining the life you want. Or seeking and creating what fulfills you and brings you joy. I hope you liked the cast of female characters and enjoyed reading about their lives, setbacks, and adventures. Many had attitudes and opportunities very different from the women of today; perhaps their wildness seems tame in a modern context, their rebellion less than outrageous, but these were women living very much in a man's world at a time when societal norms were more rigid than they are today.

Bibliography
and References

Hannah Maynard

Canadian Women Arts History Initiative. "Maynard, Hannah Hatherly,"
2007. Accessed July 23, 2019. https://cwahi.concordia.ca/sources/artists/
displayArtist.php?ID_artist=50

Forbes, Elizabeth. *Wild Roses at Their Feet: Pioneer Women of Vancouver
Island*. Vancouver: Evergreen Press Limited, 1971.

Neering, Rosemary. "An Eccentric Eye." *British Columbia Magazine*,
Winter 2006.

Royal BC Museum. "Hannah Maynard." Accessed July 23, 2019. https://
royalbcmuseum.bc.ca/exhibits/bc-archives-time-machine/galler10/
frames/maynard.htm

Wilks, Claire Weissman. *The Magic Box: The Eccentric Genius of Hannah
Maynard*. Toronto: Exile Editions Limited, 1980.

Agnes Deans Cameron

Cameron, A.D. *The New North: Being Some Account of a Woman's Journey
Through Canada to the Arctic*. New York and London: D. Appleton and
Co., 1909.

Daily Colonist. "Honored with Civic Reception: Miss Agnes Deans
Cameron Is the Central Figure in Interesting Ceremony at Alexandra
Club," December 14, 1911. Accessed August 13, 2019. https://archive.
org/stream/dailycolonist53684uvic#page/n1/mode/1up/search/
agnes+deans+cameron+new+north

Bibliography and References

———. "James K. Nesbitt Spends the Day with Women of the Gay Nineties," October 13, 1963. Accessed August 13, 2019. https://archive.org/stream/dailycolonist19631013#mode/1up/search/agnes+deans+new+north

Dickinson, Christine. "Agnes Deans Cameron," The Museum's Blog (blog). Courtenay and District Museum and Palaeontology Centre, September 21, 2012. Accessed November 2, 2018. https://www.courtenaymuseum.ca/agnes-deans-cameron

Forbes, Elizabeth. *Wild Roses at Their Feet: Pioneer Women of Vancouver Island*. Vancouver: Evergreen Press Limited, 1971.

Hale, Lynda. "Cameron, Agnes Deans." *Dictionary of Canadian Biography*, 2019. Accessed November 2, 2019. http://www.biographi.ca/en/bio/cameron_agnes_deans_14E.html

Hogg, Cameron. "A Pioneer in Education: British Columbia's Agnes Deans Cameron." *Scots in British Columbia*, 2018. Accessed November 2, 2019. https://scotsinbritishcolumbia.com/2018/03/23/a-pioneer-in-education-british-columbias-agnes-deans-cameron

McGeer, Ada. "Victoria Memories and Agnes Deans Cameron." *Daily Colonist*, October 14, 1979. Accessed August 13, 2019. https://archive.org/stream/dailycolonist19791014#page/n89/mode/1up/search/agnes+deans+cameron%E2%80%99s+cameron

Messy Nessy. "Even with a Name Like Aloha Wanderwell, You've Probably Never Heard of Her," May 15, 2018. Accessed September 26, 2019. https://www.messynessychic.com/2018/05/15/even-with-a-name-like-aloha-wanderwell-youve-probably-never-heard-of-her

Neering, Rosemary. *Wild West Women*. Vancouver: Whitecap Books, 2000.

Victoria Daily Colonist. "Amusements: Miss Cameron," December 10, 1911. Accessed November 9, 2018. http://archive.org/stream/dailycolonist53681uvic#page/n15/mode/1up

———. "Canada's Wheat Growing Area: Miss A. D. Cameron Lectures Before Full House at Victoria Theater," September 29, 1909. Accessed November 9, 2018. https://archive.org/stream/dailycolonist19090929uvic/19090929#page/n1/mode/2up

———. "My Trek to the Arctic: A Chat with Miss Agnes Deans Cameron in M.A.P.," January 27, 1910. Accessed November 9, 2019. http://archive.org/stream/dailycolonist19100227uvic/19100227#page/n29/mode/1up

———. "The Land That Never Forgets," December 19, 1911. Accessed August 13, 2019. https://archive.org/stream/dailycolonist53688uvic#page/n16/ mode/1up/search/agnes+deans+cameron+dean

VSB Archives & Heritage. "Chapter One: 1872 – 1890," June 3, 2015. Accessed November 9, 2018. http://blogs.vsb.bc.ca/heritage/2015/06/03/ chapter-one-1872-1889

Emily Carr

Beard, Hugh. "Emily Carr: A Woman of All Sorts." YouTube, uploaded by Rodney Mercer, December 9, 2016. Accessed January 19, 2019. https:// www.youtube.com/watch?v=_asBxfuCu4Q

Carr, Emily. *Growing Pains: The Autobiography of Emily Carr.* UK: Oxford University Press, 1946.

Emily Carr University of Art & Design. *Emily Carr, the Artist.* Accessed September 13, 2019. https://www.ecuad.ca/about/at-a-glance/ emily-carr-the-artist

Mason, Kerry. "What About Woo? Emily Carr's Monkey." Royal BC Museum. Accessed January 19, 2019. https://learning.royalbcmuseum.bc.ca/ wp-content/uploads/2015/06/WooPDFArticle-.pdf

Royal BC Museum. "Emily Carr Timeline." Accessed January 19, 2019. https://royalbcmuseum.bc.ca/about/explore/featured-collections/ online-emily-carr-collection/emily-carr-timeline

Silcox, David. *Emily Carr: Sister and I in Alaska.* Vancouver: Figure 1 Publishing, 2014.

Vancouver Art Gallery. *Emily Carr: A Biographical Sketch.* Accessed June 8, 2019. http://www.museevirtuel.ca/sgc-cms/expositions-exhibitions/emily_ carr/en/about/index.php

Victoria Wilson

Langston, Laura. "Louis the Parrot Lived Another 36 Years to 115, Cared for by a Servant on Retainer." *Times Colonist,* November 20, 1988.

Ruttan, Stephen. *Vancouver Island Scoundrels, Eccentrics and Originals: Tales from the Library Vault.* Victoria: TouchWood Editions, 2014.

Wylie Blanchet

Blanchet, M.W. *The Curve of Time*. Vancouver: Gray's Publishing Ltd, 1968.

Converse, Cathy. *Following the Curve of Time: The Legendary M. Wylie Blanchet*. Victoria: TouchWood Editions, 2008.

Kuhlman, Cara. "Why I Named My Boat 'Capi'" (blog entry), January 22, 2019. Accessed August 10, 2019. https://carakuhlman.com/tag/m-wylie-blanchet

Liffiton, M. "Meet M. Wylie Blanchet and Muriel W. Liffiton," January 2004. Accessed August 10, 2019. http://www.dbsparks.com/MurielLiffiton.pdf

Merriman, Alec. "Vagabond Cruising in Coastal Waters." *Daily Colonist*, July 7, 1968.

Mary Ann Gyves

Akerman, Joe. "Heal the Land, Heal the People: Strengthening Relationships at Hwaaqw'um in the Salish Sea." *Landscape Magazine*, 6(2), December 15, 2017. Accessed August 14, 2019. https://medium.com/langscape-magazine/heal-the-land-heal-the-people-1fbd62ad3e25

Kahn, Charles. *Salt Spring: The Story of an Island*. Madeira Park: Harbour Publishing, 1998.

Northwest Coach Archaeology. "Revisiting the Salt Spring Archives" (blog post), October 6, 2010. Accessed August 14, 2019. https://qmackie.com/2010/10/06/revisiting-the-salt-spring-island-archives

Roberts, Eric. *Salt Spring Saga: An Exciting Story of Pioneer Days*. Salt Spring Island: Driftwood, 1962.

Salt Spring Island Historical Society. "Amazing Women of Salt Spring Island," 2008. Accessed August 14, 2019. http://saltspringarchives.com/women.pdf

Windsor, Sheila. "St. Paul's: Salt Spring Island's First Church," *Salt Spring Island Archives*, Accessed August 7, 2019. http://saltspringarchives.com/cemetary/stpaul/index.htm

Kimiko Murakami

Bains, Camille. "Japanese Canadians Push for Apology from BC Government Over Internment Camps." Canadian Press, July 21, 2019. Accessed August 12, 2019. https://globalnews.ca/news/5664050/japanese-canadians-bc-government-apology

BC History of Nursing Society. "Rose Murakami," September 14, 2017. Accessed August 9, 2019. https://www.bcnursinghistory.ca/dvteam/rose-murakami

BC Housing. "Supportive Housing Breaks Ground on Salt Spring Island," June 1, 2007. Accessed August 9, 2019. https://www.bchousing.org/news?newsId=1479148857633

Canadian War Museum. "Forced Relocation: The Japanese-Canadian Story," 2019. Accessed August 12, 2019. https://www.warmuseum.ca/cwm/exhibitions/chrono/1931forced_e.html

Greenaway, J.E. "Kimiko Murakami: A Picture of Strength." *Salt Spring Today*, December 2005. Accessed August 9, 2019. https://www.yumpu.com/en/document/view/42842171/kimiko-murakami-salt-spring-island-archives

Kahn, Charles. *Salt Spring: The Story of an Island*. Madeira Park: Harbour Publishing, 1998.

National Post. "BC Government Apologizes for Treatment of Japanese Canadians," May 8, 2012. Accessed August 12, 2019. https://nationalpost.com/news/canada/b-c-government-apologizes-for-treatment-of-japanese-canadians

Salt Spring Island Historical Society. "Amazing Women of Salt Spring Island," 2008. Accessed August 14, 2019. http://saltspringarchives.com/women.pdf

Tofugu. "Ganbaru," 2019. Accessed August 11, 2019. https://www.tofugu.com/japanese/ganbaru

Josephine Tilden

British Columbia Parks: Ministry of Water, Land and Air Protection. "Life at the Edge." Accessed July 1, 2019. http://www.env.gov.bc.ca/bcparks/conserve/lifeattheedge.pdf

Carson, Rachel. *The Sense of Wonder: A Celebration of Nature for Parents and Children*. New York: Harper and Row, 1965.

Horsfield, Margaret. "The Enduring Legacy of Josephine Tilden." *Hakai Magazine*, June 13, 2016. Accessed June 12, 2019. https://www.hakaimagazine.com/features/enduring-legacy-josephine-tilden

Legacy.com. "Thomas David Baird Obituary," July 1, 2019. https://www.legacy.com/obituaries/timescolonist/obituary.aspx?n=thomas-david-baird&pid=127089290

Rossiter, M., Ogilvie, M., Harvey, J. *The Biographical Dictionary of Women in Science.* New York: Routledge, 2000

SeaWorld Parks & Entertainment Inc. "Intertidal Ecology." Accessed July 1, 2019. https://seaworld.org/animals/ecosystems/tide-pools/intertidal-ecology

University of Minnesota. "Josephine Tilden." Accessed June 12, 2019. https://cbs.umn.edu/about/cbs-greats/tilden

———. "Minnesota Seaside Station." Accessed July 1, 2019. http://editions.lib.umn.edu/naturalhistorymn/2013/08/27/minnesota-seaside-station

Dorothy Blackmore

Bloedel, Julius. Letter to Dorothy Blackmore, March 20, 1946. Personal collection of Patricia Currie. Accessed December 14, 2019. http://www.dorothyblackmore.com/dorothyb7.html

Currie, Patricia. "About Dorothy Blackmore." Accessed June 21, 2019. http://www.dorothyblackmore.com

———. "Re: Dorothy Blackmore story." Personal correspondence with the author, December 2, 2019.

Harbord, Heather. "Capt. Dorothy Blackmore: Pioneer Port Alberni Skipper." *Western Mariner,* June 2004, pp. 21-23.

Harlow, K.E. "A Brief Look at Tugboat History." *Harlow Marine International, Inc,* May 2013. Accessed June 21, 2019. https://www.harlowmarine.com/a-brief-look-at-tugboat-history

Knox, Jack. "A Tale of Two Captains, and a Sincere Mea Culpa." *Times Colonist,* April 14, 2019. Accessed June 21, 2019. https://www.timescolonist.com/news/local/jack-knox-a-tale-of-two-captains-and-a-sincere-mea-culpa-1.23790916

Neill, A.W. Letter to George Blackmore, January 12, 1937. Personal collection of Patricia Currie. Accessed December 14, 2019. http://www.dorothyblackmore.com/dorothyb6.html

Pacific Motor Boat. "It's Miss Captain to You, Mate!" December 1945, pp. 46-47.

Star Weekly. "Women Invade Traditional Male Domains." July 14, 1946 (Toronto, ON).

Terry, Pat. "Capt. Dorothy Blackmore of Port Alberni, Follows Dad." *Vancouver Sun,* December 6, 1937.

West Coast Advocate. "Police Boat Makes Thrilling Rescue on Stormy West Coast," March 14, 1946.

Emma Stark

Great Unsolved Mysteries in Canadian History. "Louis and Sylvia Stark," Who Killed William Robinson: Race, Justice and Settling the Land. Accessed July 27, 2019. https://www.canadianmysteries.ca/sites/robinson/murder/castofcharacters/1720en.html

Gulf Islands Driftwood. "B.C. Spells Freedom for the Estes, Starks," December 12, 1979.

Hamilton, Bea. *Salt Spring Island*. Vancouver: Mitchell Press Limited, 1969.

Kahn, Charles. *Salt Spring: The Story of an Island*. Madiera Park: Harbour Publishing, 1998.

Nanaimo Free Press. "Mrs. Stark, 106, Salt Spring Island, Ex-Slave, Passes-on," October 1944.

Poirier, Genevre. "Stark Family Landed During Black History Month." *Star*, March 1, 2006.

Salt Spring Island Archives. "Estes/Stark Family." Accessed July 27, 2019. http://saltspringarchives.com/Naidine/index.htm

Salt Spring Island Historical Society. "Amazing Women of Salt Spring Island," 2008. Accessed August 14, 2019. http://saltspringarchives.com/women.pdf

Stark-Wallace, Marie. "From Slavery to Freedom: The History of the Stark Family." *Gulf Islands Driftwood* (Salt Spring Island, BC). Ten-part series, 1979.

Aloha Wanderwell

DePrest, Jessica . "Aloha Wanderwell Baker." In Jane Gaines, Radha Vatsal, and Monica Dall'Asta, eds. Women Film Pioneers Project. New York, NY: Columbia University Libraries, 2018.

Diamond, Richard. "Re: Aloha Wanderwell Inquiry." Personal correspondence with author, September 23, 2019.

Obee, Dave. "Fearless Young Adventurer Had Roots on the Island." *Times Colonist*, November 20, 2016. Accessed August 13, 2019. https://www.timescolonist.com/entertainment/books/fearless-young-adventurer-had-roots-on-the-island-1.2943569

Richard Diamond Trust. "Aloha Wanderwell Biography," 2019. Accessed
October 23, 2018. https://www.alohawanderwell.com/biography

Rickey, Carrey. "Overlooked No More: Aloha Wanderwell, Explorer and
Filmmaker." *New York Times*, April 17, 2019. Accessed August 12, 2019.
https://www.nytimes.com/2019/04/17/obituaries/aloha-wanderwell-
overlooked.html

Treace, Dan. "The Wanderwell Expedition: Model T Fords Circle the Globe."
TModelMan.com. Accessed August 13, 2019. http://www.tmodelman.com/
wanderwell.php

Wanderwell, Aloha. *Call to Adventure!* New York: Robert M. McBride, 1939;
Rpt. as *Aloha Wanderwell: Call to Adventure*. Ed. Alan Boyd. Orange
County: Nile Baker Estate, 2013.

Wilson, Deborah. "B.C. Teenage Adventurer's Achievements 'Lost
to History.'" CBC News, November 8, 2016. Accessed October
23, 2018. https://www.cbc.ca/news/canada/british-columbia/
aloha-wanderwell-first-woman-round-the-world-driver-1.3841229

Elizabeth Quocksister

Dignity Memorial. "Captain George Quocksister." Accessed October 22,
2019. https://www.dignitymemorial.com/obituaries/campbell-river-bc/
captain-quocksister-7424990

Douglas, Kristin. "City of Campbell River Recognizes Community Leader."
Campbell River Mirror, July 16, 2016. https://www.campbellrivermirror.
com/news/city-of-campbell-river-recognizes-community-leader

Kirley, Maria. "Exhibit a Portrait of a Generation." *Campbell River Mirror*,
June 16, 2011. https://www.campbellrivermirror.com/community/
exhibit-a-portrait-of-a-generation

Museum at Campbell River. *Elizabeth Quocksister Collection*. Accessed
October 22, 2019. https://campbellriver.crmuseum.ca/category/gallery/
elizabeth-quocksister-collection

Quocksister, George. Personal interview. October 26, 2019.

Quocksister, George, and Bear, Carol. Personal interview. November 2, 2019.

Rardon, J.R. "Residential School Demolition to Help Close
Door on Dark Period." *Campbell River Mirror*, February
12, 2015. https://www.campbellrivermirror.com/news/

residential-school-demolition-to-help-close-door-on-dark-period

Wei Wai Kum First Nation. "Candidate Statement: George Quocksister Jr."
Accessed October 23, 2019. https://weiwaikum.ca/candidate-statements-2/
candidate-statement-george-quocksister-jr

———. "Our Culture." Accessed October 23, 2019. https://weiwaikum.ca/
about/our-culture

Ada Annie Rae-Arthur

Buckland, Peter. Personal interview. July 11, 2019.

Horsfield, Margaret. *Cougar Annie's Garden*. Nanaimo: Salal Books, 1999.

McIntyre, Sean. "Cougar Annie's Garden: A Remote Homestead on
Vancouver Island Is a Testament to a Pioneer Woman's Skill and
Determination." *Canada's History*, July 20, 2015. Accessed July 19, 2018.
www.canadashistory.ca/explore/women/cougar-annie-s-garden

Times Colonist. "Island's Cougar Annie Becomes a T-Shirt Icon," September
9, 2008.

Whysall, Steve. "Revisiting Cougar Annie's Garden." *Vancouver Sun*, February
25, 2016.

Ann Elmore Haig-Brown

Boyce, Beth. "Ann-Elmore Haig Brown." *Campbell River Herald*, April 24,
2019.

Campbell River and North Island Transition Society. "What We Do," 2019.
Accessed June 23, 2019. https://www.annelmorehouse.ca

Campbell River Social Planning Committee. "Ann Elmore's Legacy: Preparing
for Social Change," 2009. Accessed June 23, 2019. https://www.sparc.
bc.ca/wp-content/uploads/2017/01/campbell-river-2009-report.pdf

Haig-Brown, Roderick. *Measure of the Year: Reflections on Home, Family and
a Life Fully Lived*. Victoria: TouchWood Editions, 2011.

Haig-Brown, Valerie. *Deep Currents: Roderick and Ann Haig-Brown*. Victoria:
Orca Book Publishers, 1997.

Museum at Campbell River. "Haig-Brown Heritage House," 2014. Accessed
June 23, 2019. http://www.haig-brown.bc.ca

Bibliography and References

Lilian Bland

Belfast Telegraph. "Journalist, Photographer, Crackshot and the First Woman to Fly an Aeroplane ... The Amazing Lilian Bland," August 13, 2010.

Boland, Rosita. "Lilian Bland, the First Woman to Fly an Aircraft in Ireland." *Irish Times*, August 30, 2016. Accessed August 14, 2019. https://www.irishtimes.com/life-and-style/people/lilian-bland-the-first-woman-to-fly-an-aircraft-in-ireland-1.2765782

Daily Colonist. "Charles Bland of Quatsino Sound," November 4, 1973.

"Lilian Bland." Accessed August 14, 2019. https://reference.jrank.org/biography-2/Bland_Lilian.html

"Lilian Bland: Ireland's First Female Aviator." Accessed August 14, 2019. http://www.lilianbland.ie

McSween, Joseph. "Seagulls Inspired Woman to Build Plane." *Times Colonist*, March 20, 1965.

Memory BC. "Lilian Bland." Accessed August 7, 2019. https://www.memorybc.ca/bland-lilian-emily

North Island Gazette. "The Adventurous Life of Lilian Bland," May 11, 2016.

Williams, Claire. "Celebrating Lilian Bland on International Women's Day." University of British Columbia, March 7, 2019. Accessed August 7, 2019. https://rbsc.library.ubc.ca/2019/03/07/celebrating-lilian-bland-on-international-womens-day

Women's Museum of Ireland. "Lilian Bland: Pioneering Aviatrix." Accessed August 14, 2019. https://womensmuseumofireland.ie/articles/lilian-bland

Ga'axsta'las (Jane Constance Cook)

"Feminism." Merriam-Webster, 2019. Accessed September 1, 2019. https://www.merriam-webster.com/dictionary/feminism

Kwakiutl Band Council. "Our Culture," 2018. Accessed September 1, 2019. https://www.kwakiutl.bc.ca/our-culture

Layland, Michael. "Our History: When Capt. Cook First Found the Island." *Times Colonist*, October 3, 2014. Accessed September 1, 2019. https://www.timescolonist.com/our-history-when-capt-cook-first-found-the-island-1.1413933

Montpetit, Isabelle. "Background: The Indian Act." CBC News, May 30, 2011. Accessed September 1, 2019. https://www.cbc.ca/news/canada/background-the-indian-act-1.1056988

Neel, Ellen. "Beloved Native Lady Passed." *Native Voice*, October 1951.
Accessed September 1, 2019. http://nativevoice.ca/wp-content/
uploads/2018/07/nv-1951v10.pdf

Robertson, Leslie. *Standing Up with Ga'axsta'las: Jane Constance Cook and the Politics of Memory, Church and Custom.* Vancouver: UBC Press, 2012.

Speck, Wedlidi. Personal interview. November 18, 2019.

Union of BC Indian Chiefs. "McKenna-McBride Royal Commission,"
2019. Accessed September 15, 2019. https://www.ubcic.bc.ca/
mckenna_mcbride_royal_commission

Ellen Gibbs

Forbes, Elizabeth. *Wild Roses at Their Feet: Pioneer Women of Vancouver Island.* Vancouver: Evergreen Press Limited, 1971.

Hill, Phyllis. "Hike of Memories." *Daily Colonist*, August 2, 1970.

Peterson, Lester. *The Cape Scott Story.* Vancouver: Mitchell Press, Limited, 1974.

Silvertz, Barbara. *A History of Nanoose Bay, Second Edition.* Nanoose Volunteer Fire Department Ladies' Auxiliary, 1958.

Wells, R.E. "The Cape Scott Story: Past, Present and Future." *Daily Colonist*, May 30, 1971.

Archives

Alberni District Historical Society, Port Alberni

City of Victoria Archives, Victoria

Museum at Campbell River, Campbell River

Nanaimo Community Archives, Nanaimo

Royal BC Museum and Archives, Victoria

Salt Spring Historical Archives, Salt Spring Island

U'mista Cultural Centre, Alert Bay

University Archives and Special Collections, University of Saskatchewan, Saskatoon

University of Minnesota Archives, Minneapolis

Acknowledgements

ABUNDANT GRATITUDE TO everyone who helped bring this book from idea to existence. Thank you to Lara Kordic, Nandini Thaker, and Heritage House for supporting this project. My sincere appreciation goes to Lesley Cameron for the brilliant edits, insights, and attention to detail. Thank you to Katie Heffring for editing my initial proposal and Kristin Wenberg for the author photo.

I am grateful for the remarkable people with whom I connected while researching and writing. Thank you to the following for the assistance with research and/or photos: Cathy Bagley at the Alberni Valley Museum, Carol Bear, Janet Blanchet, Michael Blanchet, Tara Blanchet, Peter Buckland, Margaret Cadwaladr, Jennifer Claybourne at the University of Minnesota Archives, Cathy Converse, Patricia and Rob Currie, Bonnie Dahl at the University of Saskatchewan Archives, Richard Diamond (and www.alohawanderwell.com), David Hill-Turner, Juanita Johnston at U'mista Cultural Centre, Darryl MacKenzie at the City of Delta and Delta Heritage Society, John Manning, Christine Meutzner at the Nanaimo Archives, Gord Miller, Daphne Peterson, Colm O'Rourke (www.lilianbland.ie), Megan Purcell at Museum at Campbell River, George Quocksister Jr., Sarah Rathjen at the City of Victoria Archives, Leslie Robertson, Ceridwen Ross Collins at the Salt Spring Museum and Archives, Louella Serhan, Wedlidi

Speck for reviewing the note of reconciliation and the profile of Ga'axsta'las, and Kelly-Ann Turkington at the Royal BC Museum and Archives.

Thank you to all the strong women in my life who support and inspire me: Marissa Bradley, Tammy Elliott, Lara Harmon, Lauren Healey, Lynda Healey, Meghan Gillespie, Dominique Klees-Themens, Steph Kveton, Jenn Ried, Leigh Sheardown, Meaghan Valdmanis, Kristie Vergoe, and Currin Windecker. And all the women I've worked alongside while canoe tripping, guiding, tree planting, teaching, and counselling. Thank you to my healers, Lana Unger and Tonia Winchester.

An immense thank you to my parents Cathy and Michael Kuntz, who raised three determined women while modelling strength, kindness, teamwork, vulnerability, and unending support. Thank you to my sisters who are my rocks: Carmen Kuntz and Alison Martin. Thank you to my extended family, including my aunties and uncles who have always been in my life and to my Grandfather Clair Kuntz and Grandma Ione Cahill who are both resilient and inspiring. Steven Healey, thank you for the endless support and encouragement with this project, the happiness, my bikes, all the cups of tea, and for understanding me fully. I love you and our life together.

Index

Akerman, Bob, 41. *See also*
    Gyves, Mary Ann
Akerman, Joe, 41 *See also*
    Gyves, Mary Ann
activist, 105, 113, 123
advocacy, 81, 91, 109
Alabama, 56
Alaska, 10, 106
Alert Bay, 91–92, 107–9,
    112–18
Alberta, 45
    Athabasca River, 18–19
    Cardston, 46
    Lloydminster, 73
    Magrath, 45–46
Alert Bay, 91–92, 107–9,
    112, 118
Africa, 70
Anglican Church, the, 46
Arctic Ocean, 3, 18–20
Arnold, Esau, 77
Australia, 53
aviatrix, 98, 100

Baird, Tom, 49–51
Baker, Walter, 70
Bamfield, 77
Barkerville, 10
Bear, Carol, 96

Black Diamond, the, 61
Blackmore, Dorothy, 5,
    55–59
Blackmore, George, 55
Blackmore Marine Services,
    56, 58
Blanchet, Geoffrey, 34
Blanchet, M. Wylie "Capi,"
    5, 33–37
Bland, Charles, 100–2
Bland Community
    Park, 103
Bland, Lilian, 98–104
Bleriot, Louis, 99
Bloedel, Julius, 55
Bloedel, Stewart and Welch
    (company), 55
Boat Basin, 72–75, 78–80
Boat Basin Foundation, 80
    Temperate Rainforest
    Field Study Cen-
    tre, 80
Botanical Beach, 50
Bowmanville, 8
British Columbia (BC), 16,
    22, 24, 30, 37, 43–45,
    49, 55
    Cariboo, 39
    Desolation Sound, 34

Gulf Islands, 61
    Housing, 48
    University of British
        Columbia, 48
Buckland, Peter, 79–80

California, 15, 24, 60–61,
    69, 83, 102
    Long Beach, 70
    Los Angeles, 71
    Newport Beach, 71
    Sacramento, 73
    San Francisco, 23
    University of California
        at Berkeley, 81
Call to Adventure, A, 71
Campbell, George, 77
Campbell River 83, 85,
    87–93, 95–96
    Community Builder
        Award, 95
Canada, 8, 19, 43, 59, 76,
    82, 88, 92, 94, 100, 103
    Canada Post, 76
    Canadian Broadcast-
        ing Corporation
        (CBC), 59
    Canadian Pacific
        Railway, 10

Department of Trans-
  portation, 56
Government of, 4,
  46, 110
Governor General's
  Award, 27
House of Commons, 56
Merchant Marine, 58
National Archives of, 47
Royal Canadian Air
  Force, the, 58
Shipping Act, the, 56
Cape Scott, 114, 117, 119–22
Fisherman's River, 119
Guise Bay, 116, 120
North Coast Trail, 120
San Josef, 118
Shushartie Bay, 117,
  119–20
Stranby River, 120
Caprice, the, 34, 36
Carma, the, 70
Carr, Emily, 4, 15,
  22–28, 108
University of Art and
  Design, 22–23, 28
China, 69
Clark, James, 64
Clayton, *See also* Blackmore,
  Dorothy
Fishing Resort, 58–59
Coal Harbour, 100
Coast Salish, 38, 60
Commodore III, 57
Comox, 16, 71
Cook, Jane Constance.
  See Ga'axsta'las
Cook, Stephen, 107–108
Cortes Island, 34
Cougar Annie. *See* Rae-
  Arthur, Ada Annie

Cougar Annie's Garden,
  74–77
Cowichan, 38–39, 60
Culvert, Robert, 78
Curve of Time, The, 34, 37.
  See also Blanchet, M.
  Wylie "Capi"

Daily Colonist, the, 103, 118
Da'naxda'xw Nation, 91
Deans Cameron, Agnes,
  15–21
discrimination, 61, 65
Douglas, Lady Amelia Con-
  nolly, 10
Douglas, Sir James, 10, 61

Earhart, Amelia, 67, 98
Egypt, Cairo, 68
Port Said, 68
England, 8, 24, 30, 59, 73,
  82, 100–3, 114, 116
British Royal Navy, 116
English Channel, 99
Church of England, 16
Cornwall, 114
Kent, 99
London, 24
settlers, 115
entrepreneur, 7, 72
Estes, Howard, 61, 64
Europe, 59–60, 67, 76

female scientist, 51
feminist, 112, 123
First World War, 111
Florida, 54
Golden Bough
  Community, 54
Lake Wales, 54

Ford, Model T, 66, 68,
  100, 102
France, 24, 70
Marseilles, 68
Nice, 67
Paris, 66, 99
Ypres, 67
Fredericksen, Theodore,
  117, 120
*Free Land Homestead
  Act*, 115
Fort Rupert, 106
fur traders, 30

Ga'axsta'las, 5, 105–13
gender equality, 18
Germany, 99
Gibbs, Billy, 116–17, 120
Gibbs, Ellen, 114–21
Gilbert, William, 106
Gixam Clan, 106
Glendale, George, 91
Gold River, 73
gold rush, 9, 23
Gosselim, Tuwa' hwiye
  Tusium, 38–41
Grand Forks, 59
Group of Seven, the, 25, 28
*Guinness Book of World
  Records, The*, 71
Gyves, Mary Ann, 38–41, 43
Gyves, Michael, 39

Haida Gwaii, 10, 24
Haig-Brown, Ann Elmore,
  81–90
Above Tide, 81, 84,
  89–90
Bed and Breakfast, 89
Transition House, 89

Index

Haig-Brown, Roderick,
    81–87, 90
Haig-Brown, Valerie, 81, 84
Hall, Alfred, 107
Hall, Elizabeth, 106
Hall, Margaret, 69–70
Hansen, Rasmus, 117
Hawaii, 53, 60
Henderson, Katherine, 91
heredetary Chief, 91–92,
    96, 112–13
Hesquiat Harbour, 73, 75
Holberg, 118–19
Horsfield, Margaret, 74–78
Hudson Bay Company, the,
    9, 18
human rights, 48

India, 68–69
    Bombay, 68
    Calcutta, 68–69
Indian Act, the, 106
Indigenous, 18, 25, 73, 94,
    105–9, 111, 113
injustices, 5, 48
internment camp, 42,
    45–46, 48
Iowa, Davenport, 51
Ireland, 39
    Glengormley, 104
    Tipperary, 99
Italy, 88, 99
    Rome, 99

Japan, 42–44, 60, 76
    Kyoto, 70
Japanese Canadians,
    42–44, 46
    fishing floats, 119
Jensen, Nels, 117

Jervis Inlet, 34
Johnstone Strait, 94
    Bones Bay Cannery, 94
journalist, 98–100
Juan de Fuca Provincial
    Park, 50

Kelsey Bay, 92
Kentucky, 60
    Louisville, 61
Kingcome Inlet, 34, 94
Knight Inlet, 91
Kwakiutl District Coun-
    cil, 96
Kwakwala, 94–95, 106, 108
Kwakwaka'wakw, 36, 109–
    110, 112
land claims, 105
land pre-emption, 39, 51,
    62, 73

Lawson, George, 78. *See
    also* Rae-Arthur, Ada
    Annie
LeMare, Percy, 116
librarian, 81

MacMillan, Conway, 51, 53
Mackenzie River, 18
Madden, Mary, 102
Manitoba,
    Winnipeg, 67, 73
marine biologist, 49
Maxwell, John, 39
Mayfly, the, 100, 104
Maynard, Hannah, 7–14
Maynard, Richard, 8–10, 14
Mayne Island, 44
McKenna–McBride Royal
    Commission, 111

Measure of the Year, The, 87
mediator, 105
Merville, 71
Mexico, 83
midwife, 39, 91, 105, 117
Minnesota, 49–51
    Seaside Research Station,
        51–52
    University of Minnesota,
        49–51, 53
Missouri, 60
    Clay County, 61
Montreal, 56
Mount Haig-Brown, 89
Mount Maxwell, 41. *See
    also* Maxwell, John
Murakami Gardens, 48
Murakami, Katsuyori,
    43–44, 46–47
Murakami, Kimiko, 4,
    42–48
Murakami, Rose, 47–48
    Museum at Campbell
        River, 82, 93

Nanaimo, 10, 60, 64,
    114–116
    Cedar, 62
    Chase River, 62, 64–65
    Cranberry, 62
    Extension, 65
    Haliburton Street, 115
    Municipal Cemetery, 64
    Wellington coal
        mines, 116
Nanoose Bay, 115–116, 120
Nebraska, 51
Neel, Ellen, 113
Neill, A.W, 56
New North, The, 19

New Zealand, 26
New York, 26, 39
North America, 47
Nuu-chah-nulth, 23
Ohio, 51
Ontario, 8
Ottawa, 26, 47

Parksville, 115
Pearl Harbour, 44
Pennsylvania, 114
Port Alberni, 55, 57, 79
    Boat House, the, 58.
        See also Blackmore,
        Dorothy
Port Alice, 100–101
    hospital, 103
Port Hardy, 104
Port Renfrew, 49, 51, 54
potlatch, 106, 108–9, 111
Princess Maquinna, 77
professor, 50–51
progressive, 8
Public School Act, the, 16

Quadra Island, 34
Qualicum Beach, 67
Quatsino Sound, 4, 100–2
Quocksister Elizabeth, 4,
    91–97
Quocksister, George Jr., 96
Quocksister, George Sr., 92

racism, 47, 111
Rae-Arthur, Ada Annie,
    3–4, 72–80
Rae-Arthur, Willie, 73, 77
reconciliation, 6, 97
Red Army of Siberia, 70
Red Cross, the, 32, 86

reserve lands, 111
residential school, 23, 92,
    106, 112
    Indian Girls' Mission,
        107
    Indian Boys' Mission,
        107
    St. Michael's, 92, 95, 108
resilience, 81
Robertson, Leslie, 106
Rocky Mountains, the, 44
Royal BC Museum, 25

Saanichton, 61
Salish Sea, 60
Salt Spring Island, 38–40,
    43–48, 61–62, 64–65
    Burgoyne Bay, 38, 41
    Fulford Harbour, 39, 41
    Ganges Harbour, 43
    Lady Minto Hospital, 48
    Mouat's Store, 41, 43
    Sharp Road, 43–44
    St. Paul's Cemetery, 41
    St Paul's Roman Catho-
        lic Church, 41
    Vesuvius Bay, 62
San Juan Islands, 39
Saskatchewan, 77
Sayward, 92
Seattle, 49, 56, 81–84
Scotland, 15
    Glasgow, 73
Second World War, 58, 59
Serhan, Louella, 96
Seymour Inlet, 34
Sidney, 40
Skookumchuck Rapids,
    34, 37
Snaw-Naw-As Nation, 116

Snuneymuxw First
    Nation, 6
South Africa, 73
Speck, Wedlidi, 106, 113
Stark, Emma, 60–65
Stark, Louis, 60–63
Stark, Marie, 64
Stark, Sylvia, 60–62,
    64–65
steamship, 49, 73, 76, 78
Steinem, Gloria, 3, 123
Steveston, 42
Strathcona Park, 83
    Strathcona Park
        Lodge, 86

Tahiti, 53
Tasmania, 53
teacher, 60, 64–65
tetanus, 102
Times Colonist, the, 20
Tilden, Josephine, 49–54
Tippet, John, 114
Tippet, Mary Ann, 114
    Tippet House, 120
Tofino, 58, 72
translator, 105, 109, 111
tuberculosis, 23, 111

Uchuck, the, 59
Ucluelet, 23, 25, 58–59
United States, 88
    National History
        Museum, 71
University of Washing-
    ton, 81

Vancouver, 24, 42, 56,
    73–74
    General Hospital, 90

About the Author

HALEY HEALEY grew up in Muskoka Lakes, Ontario, and is a high school counsellor and Registered Clinical Counsellor. She holds a physical and health education degree, a teaching degree, and a Master of Arts degree in counselling psychology. Her interests include local history, cycling, and exploring  Vancouver Island's backcountry. She lives in Nanaimo with her husband and husky. *On Their Own Terms* is her first book. Find out more at haleyhealey.com.

Index

Hastings Camp, 44–45
Pacific National Exhibition, (PNE), 45
Stanley Park, 24
Vancouver Island, 3–6, 14, 33, 61, 65, 72, 82–83, 114, 122
   Captain George, 34
   North Island, 98, 100, 103–104, 114
   Tug and Barge, 58
Vancouver Sun, the, 87
Victoria, 7–10, 15–16, 19–20, 23, 28, 30–33, 39–40, 42, 49, 60, 78, 106, 122
   Beacon Hill Park, 8, 13

Burdett Street, 30
Chateau Victoria Hotel, 32
Empress Hotel, 43
Goldstream Park, 26
Government Street, 15, 28
Police Department, 4, 8, 13
Ross Bay Cemetery, 14, 27

Wah Wong, Yue, 32
Wanderwell, Aloha, 66–71
Wanderwell, Walter, 65, 69–70

Wanukw, Emily, 106
Washington,
   Port Townsend, 106
   Puget Sound, 106
Western Producer, the, 77
War Measures Act, the, 44
West Coast Trail, the, 49
Whale Named Henry, A, 37
Wilson, Victoria, 29–32
Winnipeg Free Press, the, 77
Wyoming, 70

Yellowstone National Park, 54
Yukon, 10